**OLD MOO**

# HOROSCOPE AND ASTRAL DIARY

# PISCES

# OLD MOORE'S

# HOROSCOPE AND ASTRAL DIARY

## PISCES

foulsham
LONDON • NEW YORK • TORONTO • SYDNEY

W. Foulsham & Co. Ltd
for Foulsham Publishing Ltd
The Old Barrel Store, Drayman's Lane, Marlow, Bucks SL7 2FF

Foulsham books can be found in all good bookshops and direct from
www.foulsham.com

ISBN: 978-0-572-04582-1

Copyright © 2015 Foulsham Publishing Ltd

A CIP record for this book is available from the British Library

Typeset in Great Britain by Chris Brewer Origination, Christchurch
Printed in Great Britain by Martins The Printers, Berwick-upon-Tweed

# CONTENTS

# INTRODUCTION

Astrology has been a part of life for centuries now, and no matter how technological our lives become, it seems that it never diminishes in popularity. For thousands of years people have been gazing up at the star-clad heavens and seeing their own activities and proclivities reflected in the movement of those little points of light. Across centuries countless hours have been spent studying the way our natures, activities and decisions seem to be paralleled by their predictable movements. Old Moore, a time-served veteran in astrological research, continues to monitor the zodiac and has produced the Astral Diary for 2016, tailor-made to your own astrological makeup.

*Old Moore's Astral Diary* is unique in its ability to get the heart of your nature and to offer you the sort of advice that might come from a trusted friend. It enables you to see in a day-by-day sense exactly how the planets are working for you. The diary section advises how you can get the best from upcoming situations and allows you to plan ahead successfully. There's also room on each daily entry to record your own observations or appointments.

While other popular astrology books merely deal with your astrological 'Sun sign', the Astral Diaries go much further. Every person on the planet is unique and Old Moore allows you to access your individuality in a number of ways. The front section gives you the chance to work out the placement of the Moon at the time of your birth and to see how its position has set an important seal on your overall nature. Perhaps most important of all, you can use the Astral Diary to discover your Rising Sign. This is the zodiac sign that was appearing over the Eastern horizon at the time of your birth and is just as important to you as an individual as is your Sun sign.

It is the synthesis of many different astrological possibilities that makes you what you are and with the Astral Diaries you can learn so much. How do you react to love and romance? Through the unique Venus tables and the readings that follow them, you can learn where the planet Venus was at the time of your birth. It is even possible to register when little Mercury is 'retrograde', which means that it appears to be moving backwards in space when viewed from the Earth. Mercury rules communication, so be prepared to deal with a few setbacks in this area when you see the sign ☿. The Astral Diary will be an interest and a support throughout the whole year ahead.

*Old Moore extends his customary greeting to all people of the Earth and offers his age-old wishes for a happy and prosperous period ahead.*

# THE ESSENCE OF PISCES

## Exploring the Personality of Pisces the Fishes

(20TH FEBRUARY – 20TH MARCH)

## What's in a sign?

Pisceans are fascinating people – everyone you come across is likely to admit that fact. By nature you are kind, loving, trustful and inclined to work very hard on behalf of the people you love – and perhaps even those you don't like very much. Your nature is sympathetic and you will do anything you can to improve the lot of those you consider to be worse off than yourself. There is a very forgiving side to your temperament and also a strong artistic flair that can find an outlet in any one of a dozen different ways.

It's true you are difficult to know, and there is a very important reason for this. Your nature goes deep, so deep in fact that someone would have to live with you for a lifetime to plumb even a part of its fathomless depths. What the world sees is only ever a small part of the total magic of this most compulsive and fascinating zodiac sign. Much of your latent power and natural magic is constantly kept bottled up, because it is never your desire to manipulate those around you. Rather, you tend to wait in the shadows until opportunities to come into your own present themselves.

In love you are ardent and sincere, though sometimes inclined to choose a partner too readily and too early. There's a dreamy quality to your nature that makes you easy to adore, but which can also cause difficulties if the practical necessities of life take a very definite second place.

The chances are that you love music and picturesque scenery, and you may also exhibit a definite fondness for animals. You prefer to live in the country rather than in the middle of a noisy and smelly town, and tend to keep a reasonably well-ordered household. Your family can easily become your life and you always need a focus for your energies. You are not at all good at feathering your own nest, unless you know that someone else is also going to benefit on the way. A little more selfishness probably would not go amiss on occasions because you are often far too willing to put yourself out wholesale for people who don't respect your sacrifices. Pisceans can be full of raging passions and are some of the most misunderstood people to be found anywhere within the great circle of the zodiac.

## Pisces resources

It is the very essence of your zodiac sign that you are probably sitting there and saying to yourself 'Resources? I have no resources'. Of course you are wrong, though it has to be admitted that a glaring self-confidence isn't likely to be listed amongst them. You are, however, a very deep thinker, and this can turn out to be a great advantage and a useful tool when it comes to getting on in life. Because your natural intuition is so strong (some people would call you psychic), you are rarely fooled by the glib words of others. Your own natural tendency to tell the truth can be a distinct advantage and a great help to you when it comes to getting on in life from a practical and financial viewpoint.

Whilst many of the signs of the zodiac tend to respond to life in an impulsive way, you are more likely to weigh up the pros and cons of any given situation very carefully. This means that when you do take action you can achieve much more success – as well as saving a good deal of energy on the way. People tend to confide in you automatically, so you are definitely at an advantage when it comes to knowing what makes your family and friends tick. At work you can labour quietly and confidently, either on your own or in the company of others. Some people would assert that Pisceans are model employees because you really do not know how to give anything less than your best.

Never underestimate the power of your instincts. Under most circumstances you are aware of the possible outcome of any given situation and should react as your inner mind dictates. Following this course inevitably puts you ahead of the game and explains why so quiet a sign can promote so many winners in life. Not that you are particularly competitive. It's much more important for you to be part of a winning team than to be out there collecting the glory for yourself.

You are dependable, kind, loving and peerless in your defence of those you take to. All of these are incredible resources when used in the correct way. Perhaps most important of all is your ability to get others on your side. In this you cannot be matched.

## Beneath the surface

Everyone instinctively knows that there is something very important going on beneath the surface of the Piscean mind, though working out exactly what it might be is a different kettle of fish altogether. The fact is that you are very secretive about yourself and tend to give very little away. There are occasions when this tendency can be a saving grace, but others where it is definitely a great disadvantage. What isn't hard to see is your natural sympathy and your desire to help those in trouble. There's no end gain here, it's simply the way you are. Your inspiration to do anything is rarely rooted in what your own prize is likely to be. In your soul you are poetical, deeply romantic and inextricably tied to the forces and cycles of the world that brought you to birth.

Despite your capacity for single-minded concentration in some matters, you are often subject to mental confusion. Rational considerations often take second place to intuitive foresight and even inspiration. Making leaps in logic isn't at all unusual for you and forms part of the way you judge the world and deal with it.

If you really want to get on in life, and to gain the most you can from your interactions with others, you need to be very truthful in your approach. Somehow or other that means finding out what is really going on in your mind and explaining it to those around you. This is never going to be an easy process, partly because of your naturally secretive ways. Actually some astrologers overplay the tendency of Pisces to keep its secrets. A great deal of the time you simply don't think you have anything to say that would interest others and you always lack confidence in your own judgements. This is a shame because you rarely proceed without thinking carefully and don't often make glaring mistakes.

Many Pisceans develop an ingrained tendency to believe themselves inadequate in some way. Once again this is something you should fight against. Knowing others better, and allowing them to get to know you, might cause you to feel less quirky or strange. Whether you realise it or not you have a natural magnetism that draws others towards you. Try to spend rather less time thinking – though without losing that Piscean ability to meditate which is central to your well-being. If you allow the fascinating world of the Piscean mind to be shared by the people you come to trust, you should become more understandable to people who really want to like you even more.

## Making the best of yourself

It must be remembered that the zodiac sign of Pisces represents two Fishes, tethered by a cord but constantly trying to break away from each other. This says a great deal about the basic Piscean nature. The inward, contemplative side of your personality is often at odds with the more gregarious and chatty qualities you also possess. Learning about this duality of nature can go at least part of the way towards dealing with it.

Although you often exhibit a distinct lack of self-confidence in your dealings with the world at large, you are, at heart, quite adept, flexible and able to cope under almost any circumstance. All that is really required in order to have a positive influence on life and to be successful is for you to realise what you are capable of achieving. Alas this isn't quite as easy as it might appear, because the introspective depths of your nature make you think too much and cause you to avoid the very actions that would get you noticed more. This can be something of a dilemma for Pisces, though it is certainly not insurmountable.

Never be afraid to allow your sensitivity to show. It is one of your greatest assets and it is part of the reason why other people love you so much – far more, in fact, than you probably realise. Your natural warmth, grace and charm are certain to turn heads on those occasions when you can't avoid being watched. The creative qualities that you possess make it possible for you to manufacture harmonious surroundings, both for yourself and for your family, who are very important to you. At the same time you recognise the practical in life and don't mind getting your hands dirty, especially when it comes to helping someone else out of a mess.

One of the best ruses Pisceans can use in order to get over the innate shyness that often attends the sign is to put on an act. Pisceans are very good natural actors and can easily assume the role of another individual. So, in your dealings with the world at large, manufacture a more confident individual, though without leaving out all the wonderful things that make you what you are now. Play this part for all you are worth and you will then truly be making the best of yourself.

## The impressions you give

There is absolutely no doubt that you are more popular, admired and even fancied than you could ever believe. Such is the natural modesty of your zodiac sign that you invariably fail to pick up on those little messages coming across from other people that say 'I think you are wonderful'. If we don't believe in ourselves it's difficult for us to accept that others think we are worth their consideration. Failing to realise your worth to the world at large is likely to be your greatest fault and needs to be corrected.

In a way it doesn't matter, when seen from the perspective of others. What they observe is a warm-hearted individual. Your magnetic personality is always on display, whether you intend it to be or not, which is another reason why you tend to attract far more attention than you would sometimes elicit. Most Pisceans are quite sexy, another quality that is bound to come across to the people you meet, at least some of whom would be willing to jump through hoops if you were to command it.

In short, what you show, and what you think you are, could be two entirely different things. If you don't believe this to be the case you need to carry out a straw poll amongst some of the people you know. Ask them to write down all your qualities as they see them. The result will almost certainly surprise you and demonstrate that you are far more capable, and loveable, than you believe yourself to be. Armed with this knowledge you can walk forward in life with more confidence and feel as content inside as you appear to be when viewed by the world at large.

People rely heavily on you. That much at least you will have noticed in a day-to-day sense. They do so because they know how well you deal with almost any situation. Even in a crisis you show your true colours and that's part of the reason why so many Piscean people find themselves involved in the medical profession. You are viewed as being stronger than you believe yourself to be, which is why everyone tends to be so surprised when they discover that you are vulnerable and inclined to worry.

## The way forward

You have a great deal to offer the world, even if you don't always appreciate how much. Although you are capable of being shy and introverted on occasions, you are equally likely to be friendly, chatty and very co-operative. You settle to just about any task, though you do possess a sense of freedom that makes it difficult for you to be cooped up in the same place for days and weeks at a stretch. You prefer the sort of tasks that allow your own natural proclivities to shine out, and you exhibit an instinctive creative tendency in almost anything you do.

Use your natural popularity to the full. People are always willing to put themselves out on your behalf, mainly because they know how generous you are and want to repay you for some previous favour. You should never be too proud to accept this sort of proffered help and must avoid running away with the idea that you are unequal to any reasonable task that you set yourself.

It's true that some of your thoughts are extremely deep and that you can get yourself into something of a brown study on occasions, which can be translated by the world around you as depression. However, you are far more stable than you probably believe yourself to be because Pisces is actually one of the toughest of the zodiac signs.

Because you are born of a Water sign it is likely that you would take great delight in living near the sea, or some other large body of water. This isn't essential to your well-being but it does feed your imagination. The vastness of nature in all its forms probably appeals to you in any case and most Pisceans love the natural world with its staggering diversity.

In love you are ardent and sincere, but you do need to make sure that you choose the right individual to suit you. Pisceans often settle for a protecting arm, but if this turns out to be stifling, trouble could follow. You would find it hard to live with anyone who didn't have at least a degree of your sensitivity, and you need a partner who will allow you to retain that sense of inner freedom that is so vital to your well-being.

Make the most of the many gifts and virtues that nature has bestowed upon you and don't be afraid to let people know what you really are. Actually establishing this in the first place isn't easy for you. Pisceans respond well to almost any form of meditation, which is not surprising because the sign of the Fishes is the most spiritually motivated zodiac sign of them all. When you know yourself fully you generate a personality that is an inspiration to everyone.

# PISCES ON THE CUSP

Old Moore is often asked how astrological profiles are altered for those people born at either the beginning or the end of a zodiac sign, or, more properly, on the cusps of a sign. In the case of Pisces this would be on the 20th of February and for two or three days after, and similarly at the end of the sign, probably from the 18th to the 20th of March. In this year's Astral Diaries, once again, Old Moore sets out to explain the differences regarding cuspid signs.

## The Aquarius Cusp – February 20th to 22nd

This tends to be a generally happy combination of signs, even if some of the people you come into contact with find you rather difficult to understand from time to time. You are quite capable of cutting a dash, as any Aquarian would be, and yet at the same time you have the quiet and contemplative qualities more typified by Pisces. You tend to be seen as an immensely attractive person, even if you are the last one in the world to accept this fact. People find you to be friendly, very approachable and good company in almost any social or personal setting. It isn't hard for you to get on with others, though since you are not so naturally quiet as Pisces when taken alone, you are slightly more willing to speak your mind and to help out, though usually in a very diplomatic manner.

At work you are very capable and many people with this combination find themselves working on behalf of humanity as a whole. Thus work in social services, hospitals or charities really suits the unique combinations thrown up by this sign mixture. Management is right up your street, though there are times when your conception of popularity takes the foremost place in your mind. Occasionally this could take the edge off executive decisions. A careful attention to detail shows you in a position to get things done, even jobs that others shun. You don't really care for getting your hands dirty but will tackle almost any task if you know it to be necessary. Being basically self-sufficient, you also love the company of others, and it is this adaptability that is the hallmark of success to Aquarian-cusp Pisceans.

Few people actually know you as well as they think they do because the waters of your nature run quite deep. Your real task in life is to let the world know how you feel, something you fight shy of doing now and again. There are positive gains in your life, brought about as a result of your adaptable and pleasing nature. Aquarius present in the nature allows Pisces to act at its best.

# The Aries Cusp – March 18th to 20th

This is a Piscean with attitude and probably one of the most difficult zodiac sign combinations to be understood, not only by those people with whom you come into contact but clearly by yourself too. If there are any problems thrown up here they come from the fact that Pisces and Aries have such different ways of expressing themselves to the world at large. Aries is very upfront, dynamic and dominant, all factors that are simply diametrically opposed to the way Pisces thinks and behaves. So the real task in life is to find ways to combine the qualities of Pisces and Aries, in a way that suits the needs of both and without becoming totally confused with regard to your basic nature.

The problem is usually solved by a compartmentation of life. For example, many people with this combination will show the Aries qualities strongly at work, whilst dropping into the Piscean mode socially and at home. This may invariably be the case but there are bound to be times when the underlying motivations become mixed, which can confuse those with whom you come into contact.

Having said all of this you can be the least selfish and most successful individual when you are fighting for the rights of others. This is the zodiac combination of the true social reformer, the genuine politician and the committed pacifist. It seems paradoxical to suggest that someone could fight tenaciously for peace, but this is certainly true in your case. You have excellent executive skills and yet retain an ability to tell other people what they should be doing, in fairly strident terms, usually without upsetting anyone. There is a degree of genuine magic about you that makes you very attractive and there is likely to be more than one love affair in your life. A steadfast view of romance may not be naturally present within your basic nature but like so much else you can 'train' this quality into existence.

Personal success is likely, but it probably doesn't matter all that much in a material sense. The important thing to you is being needed by the world at large.

# PISCES AND ITS ASCENDANTS

The nature of every individual on the planet is composed of the rich variety of zodiac signs and planetary positions that were present at the time of their birth. Your Sun sign, which in your case is Pisces, is one of the many factors when it comes to assessing the unique person you are. Probably the most important consideration, other than your Sun sign, is to establish the zodiac sign that was rising over the eastern horizon at the time that you were born. This is your Ascending or Rising sign. Most popular astrology fails to take account of the Ascendant, and yet its importance remains with you from the very moment of your birth, through every day of your life. The Ascendant is evident in the way you approach the world, and so, when meeting a person for the first time, it is this astrological influence that you are most likely to notice first. Our Ascending sign essentially represents what we appear to be, while the Sun sign is what we feel inside ourselves.

The Ascendant also has the potential for modifying our overall nature. For example, if you were born at a time of day when Pisces was passing over the eastern horizon (this would be around the time of dawn) then you would be classed as a double Pisces. As such, you would typify this zodiac sign, both internally and in your dealings with others. However, if your Ascendant sign turned out to be a Fire sign, such as Aries, there would be a profound alteration of nature, away from the expected qualities of Pisces.

One of the reasons why popular astrology often ignores the Ascendant is that it has always been rather difficult to establish. Old Moore has found a way to make this possible by devising an easy-to-use table, which you will find on page 125 of this book. Using this, you can establish your Ascendant sign at a glance. You will need to know your rough time of birth, then it is simply a case of following the instructions.

For those readers who have no idea of their time of birth it might be worth allowing a good friend, or perhaps your partner, to read through the section that follows this introduction. Someone who deals with you on a regular basis may easily discover your Ascending sign, even though you could have some difficulty establishing it for yourself. A good understanding of this component of your nature is essential if you want to be aware of that 'other person' who is responsible for the way you make contact with the world at large. Your Sun sign, Ascendant sign, and the other pointers in this book will, together, allow you a far better understanding of what makes you tick as an individual. Peeling back the different layers of your astrological make-up can be an enlightening experience, and the Ascendant may represent one of the most important layers of all.

## Pisces with Pisces Ascendant

You are a kind and considerate person who would do almost anything to please the people around you. Creative and extremely perceptive, nobody knows the twists and turns of human nature better than you do, and you make it your business to serve humanity in any way you can. Not everyone understands what makes you tick, and part of the reason for this state of affairs is that you are often not really quite 'in' the world as much as the people you encounter in a day-to-day sense. At work you are generally cheerful, though you can be very quiet on occasions, but since you are consistent in this regard, you don't attract adverse attention or accusations of being moody, as some other variants of Pisces sometimes do. Confusion can beset you on occasions, especially when you are trying to reconcile your own opposing needs. There are certain moments of discontent to be encountered which so often come from trying to please others, even when to do so goes against your own instincts.

As age and experience add to your personal armoury you relax more with the world and find yourself constantly sought out for words of wisdom. The vast majority of people care for you deeply.

## Pisces with Aries Ascendant

Although not an easy combination to deal with, the Pisces with an Aries Ascendant does bring something very special to the world in the way of natural understanding allied to practical assistance. It's true that you can sometimes be a dreamer, but there is nothing wrong with that as long as you have the ability to turn some of your wishes into reality, and this you are usually able to do, often for the sake of those around you. Conversation comes easily to you, though you also possess a slightly wistful and poetic side to your nature, which is attractive to the many people who call you a friend. A natural entertainer, you bring a sense of the comic to the often serious qualities of Aries, though without losing the determination that typifies the sign.

In relationships you are ardent, sincere and supportive, with a social conscience that sometimes finds you fighting the battles of the less privileged members of society. Family is important to you and this is a combination that invariably leads to parenthood. Away from the cut and thrust of everyday life you relax more fully, and think about matters more deeply than more typical Aries types might.

## Pisces with Taurus Ascendant

You are clearly a very sensitive type of person and that sometimes makes it rather difficult for others to know how they might best approach you. Private and deep, you are nevertheless socially inclined on many occasions. However, because your nature is bottomless it is possible that some types would actually accuse you of being shallow. How can this come about? Well, it's simple really. The fact is that you rarely show anyone what is going on in the deepest recesses of your mind and so your responses can appear to be trite or even ill-considered. This is far from the truth, as those who are allowed into the 'inner sanctum' would readily admit. You are something of a sensualist, and relish staying in bed late and simply pleasing yourself for days on end. However, you have Taurean traits so you desire a tidy environment in which to live your usually long life.

You are able to deal with the routine aspects of life quite well and can be a capable worker once you are up and firing on all cylinders. It is very important that you maintain an interest in what you are doing, because the recesses of your dreamy mind can sometimes appear to be infinitely more attractive. Your imagination is second to none and this fact can often be turned to your advantage.

## Pisces with Gemini Ascendant

There is great duality inherent in this combination, and sometimes this can cause a few problems. Part of the trouble stems from the fact that you often fail to realise what you want from life, and you could also be accused of failing to take the time out to think things through carefully enough. You are reactive, and although you have every bit of the natural charm that typifies the sign of Gemini, you are more prone to periods of self-doubt and confusion. However, you should not allow these facts to get you down too much, because you are also genuinely loved and have a tremendous capacity to look after others, a factor which is more important to you than any other. It's true that personal relationships can sometimes be a cause of difficulty for you, partly because your constant need to know what makes other people tick could drive them up the wall. Accepting people at face value seems to be the best key to happiness of a personal sort, and there are occasions when your very real and natural intuition has to be put on hold.

It's likely that you are an original, particularly in the way you dress. An early rebellious stage often gives way to a more comfortable form of eccentricity. When you are at your best, just about everyone adores you.

## Pisces with Cancer Ascendant

A deep, double Water-sign combination this, and it might serve to make you a very misunderstood, though undoubtedly popular, individual. You are anxious to make a good impression, probably too keen under certain circumstances, and you do everything you can to help others, even if you don't know them very well. It's true that you are deeply sensitive and quite easily brought to tears by the suffering of this most imperfect world that we inhabit. Fatigue can be a problem, though this is somewhat nullified by the fact that you can withdraw completely into the deep recesses of your own mind when it becomes necessary to do so.

You may not be the most gregarious person in the world, simply because it isn't easy for you to put some of your most important considerations into words. This is easier when you are in the company of people you know and trust, though even trust is a commodity that is difficult for you to find, particularly since you may have been hurt by being too willing to share your thoughts early in life. With age comes wisdom and maturity, and the older you are, the better you will learn to handle this potent and demanding combination. You will never go short of either friends or would-be lovers, and may be one of the most magnetic types of both Cancer and Pisces.

## Pisces with Leo Ascendant

You are a very sensitive soul, on occasions too much so for your own good. However, there is not a better advocate for the rights of humanity than you represent and you constantly do what you can to support the downtrodden and oppressed. Good causes are your thing and there are likely to be many in your life. You will probably find yourself pushed to the front of almost any enterprise of which you are a part because, despite the deeper qualities of Pisces, you are a natural leader. Even on those occasions when it feels as though you lack confidence, you manage to muddle through somehow and your smile is as broad as the day. Few sign combinations are more loved than this one, mainly because you do not have a malicious bone in your body, and will readily forgive and forget, which the Lion on its own often will not.

Although you are capable of acting on impulse, you do so from a deep sense of moral conviction, so that most of your endeavours are designed to suit other people too. They recognise this fact and will push much support back in your direction. Even when you come across troubles in your life you manage to find ways to sort them out, and will invariably notice something new to smile about on the way. Your sensitivity rating is massive and you can easily be moved to tears.

## Pisces with Virgo Ascendant

You might have been accused on occasions of being too sensitive for your own good, a charge that is not entirely without foundation. Certainly you are very understanding of the needs of others, sometimes to the extent that you put everything aside to help them. This would also be true in the case of charities, for you care very much about the world and the people who cling tenaciously to its surface. Your ability to love on a one-to-one basis knows no bounds, though you may not discriminate as much as you could, particularly when young, and might have one or two false starts in the love stakes. You don't always choose to verbalise your thoughts and this can cause problems, because there is always so much going on in your mind and Virgo especially needs good powers of communication. Pisces is quieter and you need to force yourself to say what you think when the explanation is important.

You would never betray a confidence and sometimes take on rather more for the sake of your friends than is strictly good for you. This is not a fault but can cause you problems all the same. Because you are so intuitive there is little that escapes your attention, though you should avoid being pessimistic about your insights. Changes of scenery suit you and travel would bring out the best in what can be a repressed nature.

## Pisces with Libra Ascendant

An Air and Water combination, you are not easy to understand and have depths that show at times, surprising those people who thought they already knew what you were. You will always keep people guessing and are just as likely to hitchhike around Europe as you are to hold down a steady job, both of which you would undertake with the same degree of commitment and success. Usually young at heart, but always carrying the potential for an old head on young shoulders, you are something of a paradox and not at all easy for totally 'straight' types to understand. But you always make an impression, and tend to be very attractive to members of the opposite sex.

In matters of health you do have to be a little careful because you dissipate much nervous energy and can sometimes be inclined to push yourself too hard, at least in a mental sense. Frequent periods of rest and meditation will do you the world of good and should improve your level of wisdom, which tends to be fairly high already. Much of your effort in life is expounded on behalf of humanity as a whole, for you care deeply, love totally and always give of your best. Whatever your faults and failings might be, you are one of the most popular people around.

## Pisces with Scorpio Ascendant

You stand a chance of disappearing so deep into yourself that other people would need one of those long ladders that cave explorers use to even find you. It isn't really your fault, because both Scorpio and Pisces, as Water signs, are difficult to understand and you have them both. But that doesn't mean that you should be content to remain in the dark, and the warmth of your nature is all you need to shine a light on the wonderful qualities you possess. But the primary word of warning is that you must put yourself on display and allow others to know what you are, before their appreciation of these facts becomes apparent.

As a server of the world you are second to none and it is hard to find a person with this combination who is not, in some way, looking out for the people around them. Immensely attractive to others, you are also one of the most sought-after lovers. Much of this has to do with your deep and abiding charm, but the air of mystery that surrounds you also helps. Some of you will marry too early, and end up regretting the fact, though the majority of people with Scorpio and Pisces will find the love they deserve in the end. You are able, just, firm but fair, though a sucker for a hard luck story and as kind as the day is long. It's hard to imagine how so many good points could be ignored by others.

## Pisces with Sagittarius Ascendant

A very attractive combination this, because the more dominant qualities of the Archer are somehow mellowed-out by the caring Water-sign qualities of the Fishes. You can be very outgoing, but there is always a deeper side to your nature that allows others to know that you are thinking about them. Few people could fall out with either your basic nature or your attitude to the world at large, even though there are depths to your nature that may not be easily understood. You are capable, have a good executive ability and can work hard to achieve your objectives, even if you get a little disillusioned on the way. Much of your life is given over to helping those around you and there is a great tendency for you to work for and on behalf of humanity as a whole. A sense of community is brought to most of what you do and you enjoy co-operation. Although you have the natural ability to attract people to you, the Pisces half of your nature makes you just a little more reserved in personal matters than might otherwise be the case. More careful in your choices than either sign taken alone, you still have to make certain that your motivations when commencing a personal relationship are the right ones. You love to be happy, and to offer gifts of happiness to others.

## Pisces with Capricorn Ascendant

You are certainly not the easiest person in the world to understand, mainly because your nature is so deep and your personality so complicated, that others are somewhat intimidated at the prospect of staring into this abyss. All the same your friendly nature is attractive, and there will always be people around who are fascinated by the sheer magnetic quality that is intrinsic to this zodiac mix. Sentimental and extremely kind, there is no limit to the extent of your efforts on behalf of a deserving world, though there are some people around who wonder at your commitment and who may ridicule you a little for your staying-power, even in the face of some adversity. At work you are very capable, will work long and hard, and can definitely expect a greater degree of financial and practical success than Pisces when taken alone. Routines don't bother you too much, though you do need regular periods of introspection, which help to recharge low batteries and a battered self-esteem. In affairs of the heart you are given to impulse, which belies the more careful qualities of Capricorn. However, the determination remains intact and you are quite capable of chasing rainbows round and round the same field, never realising that you can't get to the end of them. Generally speaking you are an immensely lovable person and a great favourite to many.

## Pisces with Aquarius Ascendant

Here we find the originality of Aquarius balanced by the very sensitive qualities of Pisces, and it makes for a very interesting combination. When it comes to understanding other people you are second to none, but it's certain that you are more instinctive than either Pisces or Aquarius when taken alone. You are better at routines than Aquarius, but also relish a challenge more than the typical Piscean would. Active and enterprising, you tend to know what you want from life, but consideration of others, and the world at large, will always be part of the scenario. People with this combination often work on behalf of humanity and are to be found in social work, the medical profession and religious institutions. As far as beliefs are concerned you don't conform to established patterns, and yet may get closer to the truth of the Creator than many deep theological thinkers have ever been able to do. Acting on impulse as much as you do means that not everyone understands the way your mind works, but your popularity will invariably see you through.

Passionate and deeply sensitive, you are able to negotiate the twists and turns of a romantic life that is hardly likely to be run-of-the-mill. In the end, however, you should certainly be able to find a very deep personal and spiritual happiness.

# THE MOON AND THE PART IT PLAYS IN YOUR LIFE

In astrology the Moon is probably the single most important heavenly body after the Sun. Its unique position, as partner to the Earth on its journey around the solar system, means that the Moon appears to pass through the signs of the zodiac extremely quickly. The zodiac position of the Moon at the time of your birth plays a great part in personal character and is especially significant in the build-up of your emotional nature.

## Sun Moon Cycles

The first lunar cycle deals with the part the position of the Moon plays relative to your Sun sign. I have made the fluctuations of this pattern easy for you to understand by means of a simple cyclic graph. It appears on the first page of each 'Your Month At A Glance', under the title 'Highs and Lows'. The graph displays the lunar cycle and you will soon learn to understand how its movements have a bearing on your level of energy and your abilities.

## Your Own Moon Sign

Discovering the position of the Moon at the time of your birth has always been notoriously difficult because tracking the complex zodiac positions of the Moon is not easy. This process has been reduced to three simple stages with Old Moore's unique Lunar Tables. A breakdown of the Moon's zodiac positions can be found from page 28 onwards, so that once you know what your Moon Sign is, you can see what part this plays in the overall build-up of your personal character.

If you follow the instructions on the next page you will soon be able to work out exactly what zodiac sign the Moon occupied on the day that you were born and you can then go on to compare the reading for this position with those of your Sun sign and your Ascendant. It is partly the comparison between these three important positions that goes towards making you the unique individual you are.

# HOW TO DISCOVER YOUR MOON SIGN

This is a three-stage process. You may need a pen and a piece of paper but if you follow the instructions below the process should only take a minute or so.

**STAGE 1** First of all you need to know the Moon Age at the time of your birth. If you look at Moon Table 1, on page 26, you will find all the years between 1918 and 2016 down the left side. Find the year of your birth and then trace across to the right to the month of your birth. Where the two intersect you will find a number. This is the date of the New Moon in the month that you were born. You now need to count forward the number of days between the New Moon and your own birthday. For example, if the New Moon in the month of your birth was shown as being the 6th and you were born on the 20th, your Moon Age Day would be 14. If the New Moon in the month of your birth came after your birthday, you need to count forward from the New Moon in the previous month. If you were born in a Leap Year, remember to count the 29th February. You can tell if your birth year was a Leap Year if the last two digits can be divided by four. Whatever the result, jot this number down so that you do not forget it.

**STAGE 2** Take a look at Moon Table 2 on page 27. Down the left hand column look for the date of your birth. Now trace across to the month of your birth. Where the two meet you will find a letter. Copy this letter down alongside your Moon Age Day.

**STAGE 3** Moon Table 3 on page 27 will supply you with the zodiac sign the Moon occupied on the day of your birth. Look for your Moon Age Day down the left hand column and then for the letter you found in Stage 2. Where the two converge you will find a zodiac sign and this is the sign occupied by the Moon on the day that you were born.

## Your Zodiac Moon Sign Explained

You will find a profile of all zodiac Moon Signs on pages 28 to 31, showing in yet another way how astrology helps to make you into the individual that you are. In each daily entry of the Astral Diary you can find the zodiac position of the Moon for every day of the year. This also allows you to discover your lunar birthdays. Since the Moon passes through all the signs of the zodiac in about a month, you can expect something like twelve lunar birthdays each year. At these times you are likely to be emotionally steady and able to make the sort of decisions that have real, lasting value.

# Moon Table I

| YEAR | JAN | FEB | MAR | YEAR | JAN | FEB | MAR | YEAR | JAN | FEB | MAR |
|------|-----|-----|-----|------|-----|-----|-----|------|-----|-----|-----|
| 1918 | 12 | 11 | 12 | 1951 | 7 | 6 | 7 | 1984 | 3 | 1 | 2 |
| 1919 | 1/31 | – | 2/31 | 1952 | 26 | 25 | 25 | 1985 | 21 | 19 | 21 |
| 1920 | 21 | 19 | 20 | 1953 | 15 | 14 | 15 | 1986 | 10 | 9 | 10 |
| 1921 | 9 | 8 | 9 | 1954 | 5 | 3 | 5 | 1987 | 29 | 28 | 29 |
| 1922 | 27 | 26 | 28 | 1955 | 24 | 22 | 24 | 1988 | 18 | 17 | 18 |
| 1923 | 17 | 15 | 17 | 1956 | 13 | 11 | 12 | 1989 | 7 | 6 | 7 |
| 1924 | 6 | 5 | 5 | 1957 | 1/30 | – | 1/31 | 1990 | 26 | 25 | 26 |
| 1925 | 24 | 23 | 24 | 1958 | 19 | 18 | 20 | 1991 | 15 | 14 | 15 |
| 1926 | 14 | 12 | 14 | 1959 | 9 | 7 | 9 | 1992 | 4 | 3 | 4 |
| 1927 | 3 | 2 | 3 | 1960 | 27 | 26 | 27 | 1993 | 24 | 22 | 24 |
| 1928 | 21 | 19 | 21 | 1961 | 16 | 15 | 16 | 1994 | 11 | 10 | 12 |
| 1929 | 11 | 9 | 11 | 1962 | 6 | 5 | 6 | 1995 | 1/31 | – | 1/30 |
| 1930 | 29 | 28 | 30 | 1963 | 25 | 23 | 25 | 1996 | 19 | 18 | 19 |
| 1931 | 18 | 17 | 19 | 1964 | 14 | 13 | 14 | 1997 | 9 | 7 | 9 |
| 1932 | 7 | 6 | 7 | 1965 | 3 | 1 | 2 | 1998 | 27 | 26 | 27 |
| 1933 | 25 | 24 | 26 | 1966 | 21 | 19 | 21 | 1999 | 16 | 15 | 16 |
| 1934 | 15 | 14 | 15 | 1967 | 10 | 9 | 10 | 2000 | 6 | 4 | 6 |
| 1935 | 5 | 3 | 5 | 1968 | 29 | 28 | 29 | 2001 | 24 | 23 | 25 |
| 1936 | 24 | 22 | 23 | 1969 | 19 | 17 | 18 | 2002 | 13 | 12 | 13 |
| 1937 | 12 | 11 | 12 | 1970 | 7 | 6 | 7 | 2003 | 3 | 1 | 2 |
| 1938 | 1/31 | – | 2/31 | 1971 | 26 | 25 | 26 | 2004 | 21 | 20 | 21 |
| 1939 | 20 | 19 | 20 | 1972 | 15 | 14 | 15 | 2005 | 10 | 9 | 10 |
| 1940 | 9 | 8 | 9 | 1973 | 5 | 4 | 5 | 2006 | 29 | 28 | 29 |
| 1941 | 27 | 26 | 27 | 1974 | 24 | 22 | 24 | 2007 | 18 | 16 | 18 |
| 1942 | 16 | 15 | 16 | 1975 | 12 | 11 | 12 | 2008 | 8 | 6 | 7 |
| 1943 | 6 | 4 | 6 | 1976 | 1/31 | 29 | 30 | 2009 | 26 | 25 | 26 |
| 1944 | 25 | 24 | 24 | 1977 | 19 | 18 | 19 | 2010 | 15 | 14 | 15 |
| 1945 | 14 | 12 | 14 | 1978 | 9 | 7 | 9 | 2011 | 4 | 3 | 5 |
| 1946 | 3 | 2 | 3 | 1979 | 27 | 26 | 27 | 2012 | 23 | 22 | 22 |
| 1947 | 21 | 19 | 21 | 1980 | 16 | 15 | 16 | 2013 | 12 | 10 | 12 |
| 1948 | 11 | 9 | 11 | 1981 | 6 | 4 | 6 | 2014 | 1/31 | – | 1 |
| 1949 | 29 | 27 | 29 | 1982 | 25 | 23 | 24 | 2015 | 19 | 20 | 19 |
| 1950 | 18 | 16 | 18 | 1983 | 14 | 13 | 14 | 2016 | 9 | 8 | 8 |

# Table 2

| DAY | FEB | MAR |
|---|---|---|
| 1 | D | F |
| 2 | D | G |
| 3 | D | G |
| 4 | D | G |
| 5 | D | G |
| 6 | D | G |
| 7 | D | G |
| 8 | D | G |
| 9 | D | G |
| 10 | E | G |
| 11 | E | G |
| 12 | E | H |
| 13 | E | H |
| 14 | E | H |
| 15 | E | H |
| 16 | E | H |
| 17 | E | H |
| 18 | E | H |
| 19 | E | H |
| 20 | F | H |
| 21 | F | H |
| 22 | F | I |
| 23 | F | I |
| 24 | F | I |
| 25 | F | I |
| 26 | F | I |
| 27 | F | I |
| 28 | F | I |
| 29 | F | I |
| 30 | – | I |
| 31 | – | I |

# Table 3

| M/D | D | E | F | G | H | I | J |
|---|---|---|---|---|---|---|---|
| 0 | AQ | PI | PI | PI | AR | AR | AR |
| 1 | PI | PI | PI | AR | AR | AR | TA |
| 2 | PI | PI | AR | AR | AR | TA | TA |
| 3 | PI | AR | AR | AR | TA | TA | TA |
| 4 | AR | AR | AR | TA | TA | GE | GE |
| 5 | AR | TA | TA | TA | GE | GE | GE |
| 6 | TA | TA | TA | GE | GE | GE | CA |
| 7 | TA | TA | GE | GE | GE | CA | CA |
| 8 | TA | GE | GE | GE | CA | CA | CA |
| 9 | GE | GE | CA | CA | CA | CA | LE |
| 10 | GE | CA | CA | CA | LE | LE | LE |
| 11 | CA | CA | CA | LE | LE | LE | VI |
| 12 | CA | CA | LE | LE | LE | VI | VI |
| 13 | LE | LE | LE | LE | VI | VI | VI |
| 14 | LE | LE | VI | VI | VI | LI | LI |
| 15 | LE | VI | VI | VI | LI | LI | LI |
| 16 | VI | VI | VI | LI | LI | LI | SC |
| 17 | VI | VI | LI | LI | LI | SC | SC |
| 18 | VI | LI | LI | LI | SC | SC | SC |
| 19 | LI | LI | LI | SC | SC | SC | SA |
| 20 | LI | SC | SC | SC | SA | SA | SA |
| 21 | SC | SC | SC | SA | SA | SA | CP |
| 22 | SC | SC | SA | SA | SA | CP | CP |
| 23 | SC | SA | SA | SA | CP | CP | CP |
| 24 | SA | SA | SA | CP | CP | CP | AQ |
| 25 | SA | CP | CP | CP | AQ | AQ | AQ |
| 26 | CP | CP | CP | AQ | AQ | AQ | PI |
| 27 | CP | AQ | AQ | AQ | AQ | PI | PI |
| 28 | AQ | AQ | AQ | AQ | PI | PI | PI |
| 29 | AQ | AQ | AQ | PI | PI | PI | AR |

AR = Aries, TA = Taurus, GE = Gemini, CA = Cancer, LE = Leo, VI = Virgo, LI = Libra, SC = Scorpio, SA = Sagittarius, CP = Capricorn, AQ = Aquarius, PI = Pisces

# MOON SIGNS

## Moon in Aries

You have a strong imagination, courage, determination and a desire to do things in your own way and forge your own path through life.

Originality is a key attribute; you are seldom stuck for ideas although your mind is changeable and you could take the time to focus on individual tasks. Often quick-tempered, you take orders from few people and live life at a fast pace. Avoid health problems by taking regular time out for rest and relaxation.

Emotionally, it is important that you talk to those you are closest to and work out your true feelings. Once you discover that people are there to help, there is less necessity for you to do everything yourself.

## Moon in Taurus

The Moon in Taurus gives you a courteous and friendly manner, which means you are likely to have many friends.

The good things in life mean a lot to you, as Taurus is an Earth sign that delights in experiences which please the senses. Hence you are probably a lover of good food and drink, which may in turn mean you need to keep an eye on the bathroom scales, especially as looking good is also important to you.

Emotionally you are fairly stable and you stick by your own standards. Taureans do not respond well to change. Intuition also plays an important part in your life.

## Moon in Gemini

You have a warm-hearted character, sympathetic and eager to help others. At times reserved, you can also be articulate and chatty: this is part of the paradox of Gemini, which always brings duplicity to the nature. You are interested in current affairs, have a good intellect, and are good company and likely to have many friends. Most of your friends have a high opinion of you and would be ready to defend you should the need arise. However, this is usually unnecessary, as you are quite capable of defending yourself in any verbal confrontation.

Travel is important to your inquisitive mind and you find intellectual stimulus in mixing with people from different cultures. You also gain much from reading, writing and the arts but you do need plenty of rest and relaxation in order to avoid fatigue.

# Moon in Cancer

The Moon in Cancer at the time of birth is a fortunate position as Cancer is the Moon's natural home. This means that the qualities of compassion and understanding given by the Moon are especially enhanced in your nature, and you are friendly and sociable and cope well with emotional pressures. You cherish home and family life, and happily do the domestic tasks. Your surroundings are important to you and you hate squalor and filth. You are likely to have a love of music and poetry.

Your basic character, although at times changeable like the Moon itself, depends on symmetry. You aim to make your surroundings comfortable and harmonious, for yourself and those close to you.

# Moon in Leo

The best qualities of the Moon and Leo come together to make you warmhearted, fair, ambitious and self-confident. With good organisational abilities, you invariably rise to a position of responsibility in your chosen career. This is fortunate as you don't enjoy being an 'also-ran' and would rather be an important part of a small organisation than a menial in a large one.

You should be lucky in love, and happy, provided you put in the effort to make a comfortable home for yourself and those close to you. It is likely that you will have a love of pleasure, sport, music and literature. Life brings you many rewards, most of them as a direct result of your own efforts, although you may be luckier than average and ready to make the best of any situation.

# Moon in Virgo

You are endowed with good mental abilities and a keen receptive memory, but you are never ostentatious or pretentious. Naturally quite reserved, you still have many friends, especially of the opposite sex. Marital relationships must be discussed carefully and worked at so that they remain harmonious, as personal attachments can be a problem if you do not give them your full attention.

Talented and persevering, you possess artistic qualities and are a good homemaker. Earning your honours through genuine merit, you work long and hard towards your objectives but show little pride in your achievements. Many short journeys will be undertaken in your life.

## Moon in Libra

With the Moon in Libra you are naturally popular and make friends easily. People like you, probably more than you realise, you bring fun to a party and are a natural diplomat. For all its good points, Libra is not the most stable of astrological signs and, as a result, your emotions can be a little unstable too. Therefore, although the Moon in Libra is said to be good for love and marriage, your Sun sign and Rising sign will have an important effect on your emotional and loving qualities.

You must remember to relate to others in your decision-making. Co-operation is crucial because Libra represents the 'balance' of life that can only be achieved through harmonious relationships. Conformity is not easy for you because Libra, an Air sign, likes its independence.

## Moon in Scorpio

Some people might call you pushy. In fact, all you really want to do is to live life to the full and protect yourself and your family from the pressures of life. Take care to avoid giving the impression of being sarcastic or impulsive and use your energies wisely and constructively.

You have great courage and you invariably achieve your goals by force of personality and sheer effort. You are fond of mystery and are good at predicting the outcome of situations and events. Travel experiences can be beneficial to you.

You may experience problems if you do not take time to examine your motives in a relationship, and also if you allow jealousy, always a feature of Scorpio, to cloud your judgement.

## Moon in Sagittarius

The Moon in Sagittarius helps to make you a generous individual with humanitarian qualities and a kind heart. Restlessness may be intrinsic as your mind is seldom still. Perhaps because of this, you have a need for change that could lead you to several major moves during your adult life. You are not afraid to stand your ground when you know your judgement is right, you speak directly and have good intuition.

At work you are quick, efficient and versatile and so you make an ideal employee. You need work to be intellectually demanding and do not enjoy tedious routines.

In relationships, you anger quickly if faced with stupidity or deception, though you are just as quick to forgive and forget. Emotionally, there are times when your heart rules your head.

# Moon in Capricorn

The Moon in Capricorn makes you popular and likely to come into the public eye in some way. The watery Moon is not entirely comfortable in the Earth sign of Capricorn and this may lead to some difficulties in the early years of life. An initial lack of creative ability and indecision must be overcome before the true qualities of patience and perseverance inherent in Capricorn can show through.

You have good administrative ability and are a capable worker, and if you are careful you can accumulate wealth. But you must be cautious and take professional advice in partnerships, as you are open to deception. You may be interested in social or welfare work, which suit your organisational skills and sympathy for others.

# Moon in Aquarius

The Moon in Aquarius makes you an active and agreeable person with a friendly, easy-going nature. Sympathetic to the needs of others, you flourish in a laid-back atmosphere. You are broad-minded, fair and open to suggestion, although sometimes you have an unconventional quality which others can find hard to understand.

You are interested in the strange and curious, and in old articles and places. You enjoy trips to these places and gain much from them. Political, scientific and educational work interests you and you might choose a career in science or technology.

Money-wise, you make gains through innovation and concentration and Lunar Aquarians often tackle more than one job at a time. In love you are kind and honest.

# Moon in Pisces

You have a kind, sympathetic nature, somewhat retiring at times, but you always take account of others' feelings and help when you can.

Personal relationships may be problematic, but as life goes on you can learn from your experiences and develop a better understanding of yourself and the world around you.

You have a fondness for travel, appreciate beauty and harmony and hate disorder and strife. You may be fond of literature and would make a good writer or speaker yourself. You have a creative imagination and may come across as an incurable romantic. You have strong intuition, maybe bordering on a mediumistic quality, which sets you apart from the mass. You may not be rich in cash terms, but your personal gifts are worth more than gold.

# PISCES IN LOVE

**D**iscover how compatible in love you are with people from the same and other signs of the zodiac. Five stars equals a match made in heaven!

## Pisces meets Pisces

Pisceans are easy-going and get on well with most people, so when two Pisceans get together, harmony is invariably the result. While this isn't the most dynamic relationship, there is mutual understanding, and a desire to please on both sides. Neither partner is likely to be overbearing or selfish. Family responsibilities should be happily shared and home surroundings will be comfortable, but never pretentious. One of the better pairings for the sign of the Fishes. Star rating: * * * * *

## Pisces meets Aries

Still waters run deep, and they don't come much deeper than Pisces. Although these signs share the same quadrant of the zodiac, they have little in common. Pisces is a dreamer, a romantic idealist with steady and spiritual goals. Aries needs to be on the move, and has very different ideals. It's hard to see how a relationship could develop but, with patience, there is a chance that things might work out. Pisces needs incentive, and Aries may be the sign to offer it. Star rating: * *

## Pisces meets Taurus

No problem here, unless both parties come from the quieter side of their respective signs. Most of the time Taurus and Pisces would live comfortably together, offering mutual support and deep regard. Taurus can offer the personal qualities that Pisces craves, whilst Pisces understands and copes with the Bull's slightly stubborn qualities. Taurus is likely to travel in Piscean company, so there is a potential for wide-ranging experiences and variety which is essential. There will be some misunderstandings, mainly because Pisces is so deep, but that won't prevent their enduring happiness. Star rating: * * *

## Pisces meets Gemini

Gemini likes to think of itself as intuitive and intellectual, but it will never understand Pisces' dark depths. Another stumbling block is that both Gemini and Pisces are 'split' signs – the Twins and the two Fishes – which means that both are capable of dual personalities. There won't be any shortage of affection, but the real question has to be how much these people feel they have in common. Pisces is extremely kind, and so is Gemini most of the time. But Pisces does too much soul-searching for Gemini, who might eventually become bored. Star rating: ★★★

## Pisces meets Cancer

This is likely to be a very successful match. Cancer and Pisces are both Water signs, both deep, sensitive and very caring. Pisces loves deeply, and Cancer wants to be loved. There will be few fireworks here, and a very quiet house. But that doesn't mean that either love or action is lacking – the latter of which is just behind closed doors. Family and children are important to both signs and both are prepared to work hard, but Pisces is the more restless of the two and needs the support and security that Cancer offers. Star rating: ★★★★★

## Pisces meets Leo

Pisces always needs to understand others, which makes Leo feel warm and loved, while Leo sees, to its delight, that Pisces needs to be protected and taken care of. Pisceans are often lacking in self-confidence which is something Leo has to spare, and happily it is often infectious. Pisces' inevitable cares are swept away on a tide of Leonine cheerfulness. This couple's home would be cheerful and full of love, which is beneficial to all family members. This is not a meeting of minds, but rather an understanding and appreciation of differences. Star rating: ★★★★

## Pisces meets Virgo

This looks an unpromising match from beginning to end. There are exceptions to every rule, particularly where Pisces is concerned, but these two signs are both so deep it's hard to imagine that they could ever find what makes the other tick. The depth is different in each case: Virgo's ruminations are extremely materialistic, while Pisces exists in a world of deep-felt, poorly expressed emotion. Pisces and Virgo might find they don't talk much, so only in a contemplative, almost monastic, match would they ever get on. Still, in a vast zodiac, anything is possible. Star rating: **

## Pisces meets Libra

Libra and Pisces can be extremely fond of each other, even deeply in love, but this alone isn't a stable foundation for long-term success. Pisces is extremely deep and doesn't even know itself very well. Libra may initially find this intriguing but will eventually feel frustrated at being unable to understand the Piscean's emotional and personal feelings. Pisces can be jealous and may find Libra's flightiness difficult, which Libra can't stand. They are great friends and they may make it to the romantic stakes, but when they get there a great deal of effort will be necessary. Star rating: ***

## Pisces meets Scorpio

If ever there were two zodiac signs that have a total rapport, it has to be Scorpio and Pisces. They share very similar needs: they are not gregarious and are happy with a little silence, good music and time to contemplate the finer things in life, and both are attracted to family life. Apart, they can have a tendency to wander in a romantic sense, but this is reduced when they come together. They are deep, firm friends who enjoy each other's company and this must lead to an excellent chance of success. These people are surely made for each other! Star rating: *****

## Pisces meets Sagittarius

Probably the least likely success story for either sign, which is why it scores so low on the star rating. The basic problem is an almost total lack of understanding. A successful relationship needs empathy and progress towards a shared goal but, although both are eager to please, Pisces is too deep and Sagittarius too flighty – they just don't belong on the same planet! As pals, they have more in common and so a friendship is the best hope of success and happiness. Star rating: *

## Pisces meets Capricorn

There is some chance of a happy relationship here, but it will need work on both sides. Capricorn is a go-getter, but likes to plan long term. Pisces is naturally more immediate, but has enough intuition to understand the Goat's thinking. Both have patience, but it will usually be Pisces who chooses to play second fiddle. The quiet nature of both signs might be a problem, as someone will have to take the lead, especially in social situations. Both signs should recognise this fact and accommodate it. Star rating: ***

## Pisces meets Aquarius

Zodiac signs that follow each other often have something in common, but this is often not the case with Aquarius and Pisces. Both signs are deeply caring, but in different ways. Pisces is one of the deepest zodiac signs, and Aquarius simply isn't prepared to embark on the journey. Pisceans, meanwhile, would probably find Aquarians superficial and even flippant. On the positive side, there is potential for a well-balanced relationship, but unless one party is untypical of their zodiac sign, it often doesn't get started. Star rating: **

# VENUS:
# THE PLANET OF LOVE

If you look up at the sky around sunset or sunrise you will often see Venus in close attendance to the Sun. It is arguably one of the most beautiful sights of all and there is little wonder that historically it became associated with the goddess of love. But although Venus does play an important part in the way you view love and in the way others see you romantically, this is only one of the spheres of influence that it enjoys in your overall character.

Venus has a part to play in the more cultured side of your life and has much to do with your appreciation of art, literature, music and general creativity. Even the way you look is responsive to the part of the zodiac that Venus occupied at the start of your life, though this fact is also down to your Sun sign and Ascending sign. If, at the time you were born, Venus occupied one of the more gregarious zodiac signs, you will be more likely to wear your heart on your sleeve, as well as to be more attracted to entertainment, social gatherings and good company. If on the other hand Venus occupied a quiet zodiac sign at the time of your birth, you would tend to be more retiring and less willing to shine in public situations.

It's good to know what part the planet Venus plays in your life, for it can have a great bearing on the way you appear to the rest of the world and since we all have to mix with others, you can learn to make the very best of what Venus has to offer you.

One of the great complications in the past has always been trying to establish exactly what zodiac position Venus enjoyed when you were born, because the planet is notoriously difficult to track. However, I have solved that problem by creating a table that is exclusive to your Sun sign, which you will find on the following page.

Establishing your Venus sign could not be easier. Just look up the year of your birth on the page opposite and you will see a sign of the zodiac. This was the sign that Venus occupied in the period covered by your sign in that year. If Venus occupied more than one sign during the period, this is indicated by the date on which the sign changed, and the name of the new sign. For instance, if you were born in 1940, Venus was in Aries until the 9th March, after which time it was in Taurus. If you were born before 9th March your Venus sign is Aries, if you were born on or after 9th March, your Venus sign is Taurus. Once you have established the position of Venus at the time of your birth, you can then look in the pages which follow to see how this has a bearing on your life as a whole.

1918 AQUARIUS
1919 PISCES / 27.2 ARIES
1920 CAPRICORN /
    24.2 AQUARIUS / 19.3 PISCES
1921 ARIES / 8.3 TAURUS
1922 PISCES / 14.3 ARIES
1923 CAPRICORN
1924 ARIES / 10.3 TAURUS
1925 AQUARIUS / 4.3 PISCES
1926 AQUARIUS
1927 PISCES / 26.2 ARIES
1928 CAPRICORN /
    23.2 AQUARIUS / 18.3 PISCES
1929 ARIES / 9.3 TAURUS
1930 PISCES / 13.3 ARIES
1931 CAPRICORN
1932 ARIES / 9.3 TAURUS
1933 AQUARIUS / 4.3 PISCES
1934 AQUARIUS
1935 PISCES / 25.2 ARIES
1936 CAPRICORN /
    23.2 AQUARIUS / 18.3 PISCES
1937 ARIES / 10.3 TAURUS
1938 PISCES / 12.3 ARIES
1939 CAPRICORN
1940 ARIES / 9.3 TAURUS
1941 AQUARIUS / 3.3 PISCES
1942 AQUARIUS
1943 PISCES / 25.2 ARIES
1944 CAPRICORN /
    22.2 AQUARIUS / 18.3 PISCES
1945 ARIES / 11.3 TAURUS
1946 PISCES / 11.3 ARIES
1947 CAPRICORN
1948 ARIES / 8.3 TAURUS
1949 AQUARIUS / 3.3 PISCES
1950 AQUARIUS
1951 PISCES / 24.2 ARIES
1952 CAPRICORN /
    22.2 AQUARIUS / 17.3 PISCES
1953 ARIES
1954 PISCES / 11.3 ARIES
1955 CAPRICORN
1956 ARIES / 8.3 TAURUS
1957 AQUARIUS / 2.3 PISCES
1958 CAPRICORN /
    25.2 AQUARIUS
1959 PISCES / 24.2 ARIES
1960 CAPRICORN /
    21.2 AQUARIUS / 17.3 PISCES
1961 ARIES
1962 PISCES / 10.3 ARIES
1963 CAPRICORN
1964 ARIES / 8.3 TAURUS
1965 AQUARIUS / 1.3 PISCES
1966 AQUARIUS
1967 PISCES / 23.2 ARIES

1968 SAGITTARIUS /
    26.1 CAPRICORN
1969 ARIES
1970 PISCES / 10.3 ARIES
1971 CAPRICORN
1972 ARIES / 7.3 TAURUS
1973 AQUARIUS / 1.3 PISCES
1974 CAPRICORN / 2.3 AQUARIUS
1975 PISCES / 23.2 ARIES
1976 SAGITTARIUS /
    26.1 CAPRICORN
1977 ARIES
1978 PISCES / 9.3 ARIES
1979 CAPRICORN
1980 ARIES / 7.3 TAURUS
1981 AQUARIUS / 28.2 PISCES
1982 CAPRICORN / 4.3 AQUARIUS
1983 PISCES / 23.2 ARIES
1984 SAGITTARIUS /
    25.1 CAPRICORN
1985 ARIES
1986 PISCES / 9.3 ARIES
1987 CAPRICORN
1988 ARIES / 7.3 TAURUS
1989 AQUARIUS / 28.2 PISCES
1990 CAPRICORN / 5.3 AQUARIUS
1991 PISCES / 22.2 ARIES /
    20.3 TAURUS
1992 SAGITTARIUS /
    25.1 CAPRICORN
1993 ARIES
1994 PISCES / 9.3 ARIES
1995 CAPRICORN
1996 ARIES / 7.3 TAURUS
1997 AQUARIUS / 27.2 PISCES
1998 CAPRICORN / 5.3 AQUARIUS
1999 PISCES / 22.2 ARIES /
    19.3 TAURUS
2000 SAGITTARIUS /
    25.1 CAPRICORN
2001 ARIES
2002 PISCES / 9.3 ARIES
2003 CAPRICORN
2004 ARIES / 7.3 TAURUS
2005 AQUARIUS / 27.2 PISCES
2006 CAPRICORN / 5.3 AQUARIUS
2007 PISCES / 22.2 ARIES
2008 SAGITTARIUS /
    25.1 CAPRICORN
2009 ARIES
2010 PISCES / 9.3 ARIES
2011 CAPRICORN
2012 ARIES / 7.3 TAURUS
2013 AQUARIUS / 27.2 PISCES
2014 AQUARIUS / 27.2 PISCES
2015 PISCES / 22.2 ARIES
2016 AQUARIUS / 6.2 PISCES

# VENUS THROUGH THE ZODIAC SIGNS

## Venus in Aries

Amongst other things, the position of Venus in Aries indicates a fondness for travel, music and all creative pursuits. Your nature tends to be affectionate and you would try not to create confusion or difficulty for others if it could be avoided. Many people with this planetary position have a great love of the theatre, and mental stimulation is of the greatest importance. Early romantic attachments are common with Venus in Aries, so it is very important to establish a genuine sense of romantic continuity. Early marriage is not recommended, especially if it is based on sympathy. You may give your heart a little too readily on occasions.

## Venus in Taurus

You are capable of very deep feelings and your emotions tend to last for a very long time. This makes you a trusting partner and lover, whose constancy is second to none. In life you are precise and careful and always try to do things the right way. Although this means an ordered life, which you are comfortable with, it can also lead you to be rather too fussy for your own good. Despite your pleasant nature, you are very fixed in your opinions and quite able to speak your mind. Others are attracted to you and historical astrologers always quoted this position of Venus as being very fortunate in terms of marriage. However, if you find yourself involved in a failed relationship, it could take you a long time to trust again.

## Venus in Gemini

As with all associations related to Gemini, you tend to be quite versatile, anxious for change and intelligent in your dealings with the world at large. You may gain money from more than one source but you are equally good at spending it. There is an inference here that you are a good communicator, via either the written or the spoken word, and you love to be in the company of interesting people. Always on the look-out for culture, you may also be very fond of music, and love to indulge the curious and cultured side of your nature. In romance you tend to have more than one relationship and could find yourself associated with someone who has previously been a friend or even a distant relative.

## Venus in Cancer

You often stay close to home because you are very fond of family and enjoy many of your most treasured moments when you are with those you love. Being naturally sympathetic, you will always do anything you can to support those around you, even people you hardly know at all. This charitable side of your nature is your most noticeable trait and is one of the reasons why others are naturally so fond of you. Being receptive and in some cases even psychic, you can see through to the soul of most of those with whom you come into contact. You may not commence too many romantic attachments but when you do give your heart, it tends to be unconditionally.

## Venus in Leo

It must become quickly obvious to almost anyone you meet that you are kind, sympathetic and yet determined enough to stand up for anyone or anything that is truly important to you. Bright and sunny, you warm the world with your natural enthusiasm and would rarely do anything to hurt those around you, or at least not intentionally. In romance you are ardent and sincere, though some may find your style just a little overpowering. Gains come through your contacts with other people and this could be especially true with regard to romance, for love and money often come hand in hand for those who were born with Venus in Leo. People claim to understand you, though you are more complex than you seem.

## Venus in Virgo

Your nature could well be fairly quiet no matter what your Sun sign might be, though this fact often manifests itself as an inner peace and would not prevent you from being basically sociable. Some delays and even the odd disappointment in love cannot be ruled out with this planetary position, though it's a fact that you will usually find the happiness you look for in the end. Catapulting yourself into romantic entanglements that you know to be rather ill-advised is not sensible, and it would be better to wait before you committed yourself exclusively to any one person. It is the essence of your nature to serve the world at large and through doing so it is possible that you will attract money at some stage in your life.

## Venus in Libra

Venus is very comfortable in Libra and bestows upon those people who have this planetary position a particular sort of kindness that is easy to recognise. This is a very good position for all sorts of friendships and also for romantic attachments that usually bring much joy into your life. Few individuals with Venus in Libra would avoid marriage and since you are capable of great depths of love, it is likely that you will find a contented personal life. You like to mix with people of integrity and intelligence but don't take kindly to scruffy surroundings or work that means getting your hands too dirty. Careful speculation, good business dealings and money through marriage all seem fairly likely.

## Venus in Scorpio

You are quite open and tend to spend money quite freely, even on those occasions when you don't have very much. Although your intentions are always good, there are times when you get yourself in to the odd scrape and this can be particularly true when it comes to romance, which you may come to late or from a rather unexpected direction. Certainly you have the power to be happy and to make others contented on the way, but you find the odd stumbling block on your journey through life and it could seem that you have to work harder than those around you. As a result of this, you gain a much deeper understanding of the true value of personal happiness than many people ever do, and are likely to achieve true contentment in the end.

## Venus in Sagittarius

You are lighthearted, cheerful and always able to see the funny side of any situation. These facts enhance your popularity, which is especially high with members of the opposite sex. You should never have to look too far to find romantic interest in your life, though it is just possible that you might be too willing to commit yourself before you are certain that the person in question is right for you. Part of the problem here extends to other areas of life too. The fact is that you like variety in everything and so can tire of situations that fail to offer it. All the same, if you choose wisely and learn to understand your restless side, then great happiness can be yours.

# Venus in Capricorn

The most notable trait that comes from Venus in this position is that it makes you trustworthy and able to take on all sorts of responsibilities in life. People are instinctively fond of you and love you all the more because you are always ready to help those who are in any form of need. Social and business popularity can be yours and there is a magnetic quality to your nature that is particularly attractive in a romantic sense. Anyone who wants a partner for a lover, a spouse and a good friend too would almost certainly look in your direction. Constancy is the hallmark of your nature and unfaithfulness would go right against the grain. You might sometimes be a little too trusting.

# Venus in Aquarius

This location of Venus offers a fondness for travel and a desire to try out something new at every possible opportunity. You are extremely easy to get along with and tend to have many friends from varied backgrounds, classes and inclinations. You like to live a distinct sort of life and gain a great deal from moving about, both in a career sense and with regard to your home. It is not out of the question that you could form a romantic attachment to someone who comes from far away or be attracted to a person of a distinctly artistic and original nature. What you cannot stand is jealousy, for you have friends of both sexes and would want to keep things that way.

# Venus in Pisces

The first thing people tend to notice about you is your wonderful, warm smile. Being very charitable by nature you will do anything to help others, even if you don't know them well. Much of your life may be spent sorting out situations for other people, but it is very important to feel that you are living for yourself too. In the main, you remain cheerful, and tend to be quite attractive to members of the opposite sex. Where romantic attachments are concerned, you could be drawn to people who are significantly older or younger than yourself or to someone with a unique career or point of view. It might be best for you to avoid marrying whilst you are still very young.

# HOW THE DIAGRAMS WORK

Through the picture diagrams in the Astral Diary I want to help you to plot your year. With them you can see where the positive and negative aspects will be found in each month. To make the most of them, all you have to do is remember where and when!

Let me show you how they work ...

## THE MONTH AT A GLANCE

Just as there are twelve separate zodiac signs, so astrologers believe that each sign has twelve separate aspects to life. Each of the twelve segments relates to a different personal aspect. I list them all every month so that their meanings are always clear.

YOUR MONTH AT A GLANCE

(+) = Opportunities are around    (−) = Be on the defensive    = Life is pretty ordinary

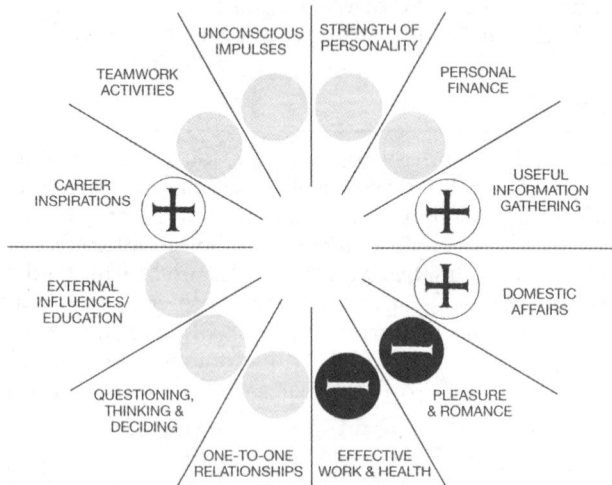

UNCONSCIOUS IMPULSES

STRENGTH OF PERSONALITY

TEAMWORK ACTIVITIES

PERSONAL FINANCE

CAREER INSPIRATIONS

USEFUL INFORMATION GATHERING

EXTERNAL INFLUENCES/ EDUCATION

DOMESTIC AFFAIRS

QUESTIONING, THINKING & DECIDING

PLEASURE & ROMANCE

ONE-TO-ONE RELATIONSHIPS

EFFECTIVE WORK & HEALTH

I have designed this chart to show you how and when these twelve different aspects are being influenced throughout the year. When there is a shaded circle, nothing out of the ordinary is to be expected. However, when a circle turns white with a plus sign, the influence is positive. Where the circle is black with a minus sign, it is a negative.

# YOUR ENERGY RHYTHM CHART

Below is a picture diagram in which I link your zodiac group to the rhythm of the Moon. In doing this I have calculated when you will be gaining strength from its influence and equally when you may be weakened by it.

If you think of yourself as being like the tides of the ocean then you may understand how your own energies must also rise and fall. And if you understand how it works and when it is working, then you can better organise your activities to achieve more and get things done more easily.

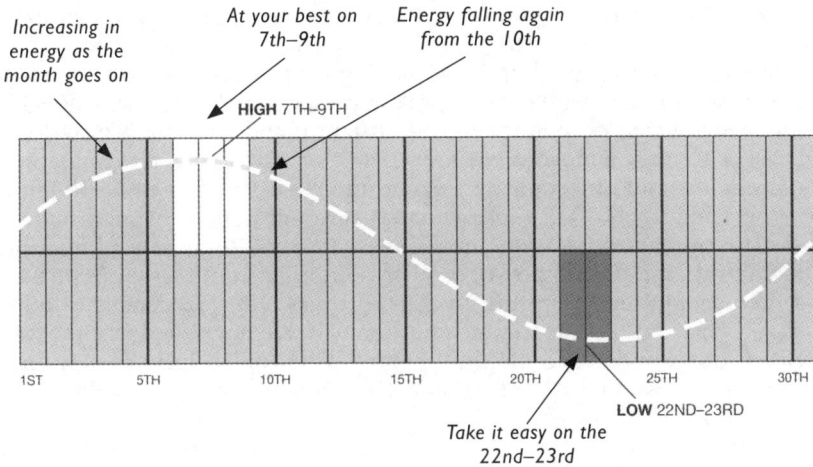

*Increasing in energy as the month goes on*

*At your best on 7th–9th*

*Energy falling again from the 10th*

**HIGH** 7TH–9TH

1ST   5TH   10TH   15TH   20TH   25TH   30TH

**LOW** 22ND–23RD

*Take it easy on the 22nd–23rd*

# THE KEY DAYS

Some of the entries are in **bold**, which indicates the working of astrological cycles in your life. Look out for them each week as they are the best days to take action or make decisions. The daily text tells you which area of your life to focus on.

# MERCURY RETROGRADE

The Mercury symbol (☿) indicates that Mercury is retrograde on that day. Since Mercury governs communication, the fact that it appears to be moving backwards when viewed from the Earth at this time should warn you that your communication skills are not likely to be at their best and you could expect some setbacks.

# PISCES: YOUR YEAR IN BRIEF

Expect a good start to the year and a time during which many of the plans you put on hold late last year will finally come to fruition. January and February give you the chance to work at your full potential and you will be happy to see that others are taking certain situations as seriously as you do. Keep in touch with people you know are in a good position to lend you some timely assistance. February should also be good on the financial front.

March and April should find you moving forward progressively on most fronts. Take extra care with regard to relationships, mainly because of possible misunderstandings. Keep in touch with distant friends and don't turn down the chance to make a move at work, even if this means a total reorganisation. Socially, you should be enjoying a varied time and will be getting to know some new and significant people who may turn out to be very important.

As the summer begins you are likely to be keen to get ahead in many different ways and your improved level of energy and enthusiasm during May and June should see an up-turn in your fortunes. Not everyone is working on your behalf at this time so watch out that you are not duped in some way. Turn on your intuition and all should be well. You won't achieve perfection at this time but you could come fairly close and that should be a good incentive to your efforts.

During July and August take care over fine details. Most aspects of life ought to be going your way but there can be complications if you leave things to chance. It would be better to repeat important tasks than to risk losing out so take any assistance offered by colleagues and friends. This is a time when you will want to be out and about, enjoying yourself in the best company and making a positive impression.

September and October could so easily bring you closer to your heart's desire. With a great sense of purpose and an instinctive knowledge as to how you should approach people and situations, very little is likely to hold you back. New promises are made and you could become involved in some new and potentially important group involvement that will go on and on far into the future.

The final months of 2016, November and December, seem especially helpful and can bring you much of what you want. November, especially, offers much and with the Sun in a positive position you will take life by the scruff of the neck and make it work for you. December may be just a little quieter. There are gains to be made in a financial sense and more excitement and upheaval around Christmas than you might have expected.

# January

2016

## YOUR MONTH AT A GLANCE

(+) = Opportunities are around  ● = Be on the defensive  ● = Life is pretty ordinary

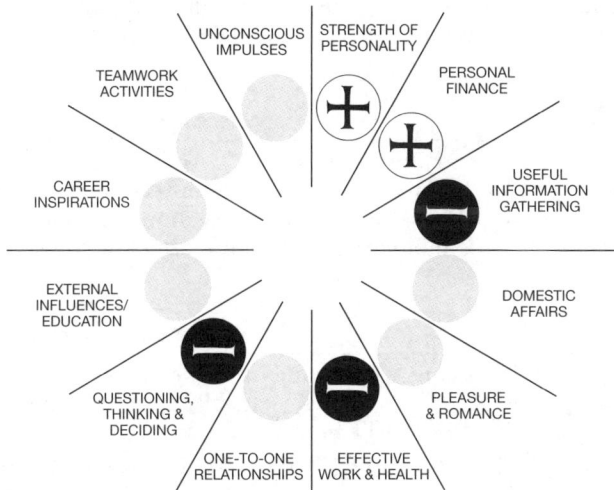

STRENGTH OF PERSONALITY
PERSONAL FINANCE
UNCONSCIOUS IMPULSES
TEAMWORK ACTIVITIES
CAREER INSPIRATIONS
USEFUL INFORMATION GATHERING
EXTERNAL INFLUENCES/ EDUCATION
DOMESTIC AFFAIRS
QUESTIONING, THINKING & DECIDING
PLEASURE & ROMANCE
ONE-TO-ONE RELATIONSHIPS
EFFECTIVE WORK & HEALTH

## JANUARY HIGHS AND LOWS

*Here I show you how the rhythms of the Moon will affect you this month. Like the tide, your energies and abilities will rise and fall with its pattern. When it is above the centre line, go for it, when it is below, you should be resting.*

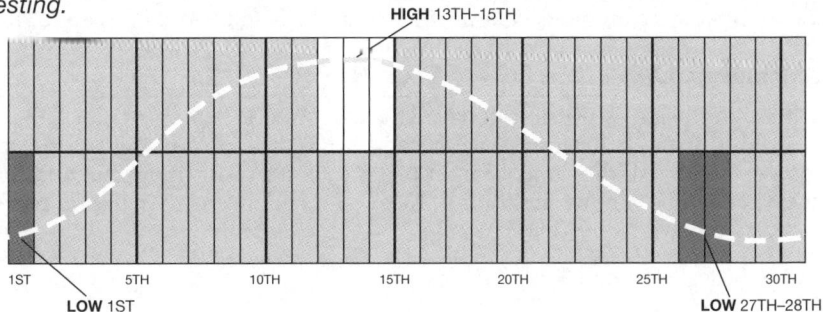

HIGH 13TH–15TH

1ST    5TH    10TH    15TH    20TH    25TH    30TH

LOW 1ST

LOW 27TH–28TH

## 1 FRIDAY
*Moon Age Day 21    Moon Sign Virgo*

The first day of the year brings new opportunities, and you want to do all you can to follow these up. You will take inspiration from anything cultured, old or unusual. With a greater than average commitment to the community in which you live this could be the time to seek out new projects.

## 2 SATURDAY
*Moon Age Day 22    Moon Sign Libra*

Your caring spirit is really on display at the moment – not that there is anything particularly unusual about that. You offer both your advice and your practical help to family members and also just about anyone you sense is in need. Be careful not to accidentally get on the wrong side of someone's pride.

## 3 SUNDAY
*Moon Age Day 23    Moon Sign Libra*

Capitalise on new potential around now. It's likely that you will discover talents you didn't even know you had and though you often lack confidence in yourself you should find that you get on swimmingly. Not everyone is equally supportive at the moment but when it matters the most, people will come good.

## 4 MONDAY
*Moon Age Day 24    Moon Sign Scorpio*

The start of a new working week brings a vigorous mood and plenty of assistance when you need it the most. Generally speaking you are jogging along quite nicely but there will be one or two people around who are difficult to weigh up. Your intuition remains strong enough to get you through most situations.

## 5 TUESDAY
*Moon Age Day 25    Moon Sign Scorpio*

Look out for an expansion of social opportunities. You seem to be in the right frame of mind to develop new interests and you are also likely to be more intrepid than might sometimes be the case. Plan now for a very special sort of holiday that comes later in the year and consult loved ones about it.

## 6 WEDNESDAY ☿
*Moon Age Day 26    Moon Sign Scorpio*

A little confusion is possible today. The chances are that this comes about as a result of the behaviour of others and it has little or nothing to do with you personally. All the same it might be up to you to sort things out and this diversion can be slightly frustrating. Keep your patience with irritating types.

## 7 THURSDAY  ☿  *Moon Age Day 27  Moon Sign Sagittarius*

Your horizons are being broadened all the time and you could now have your sights set on a possible alteration to your working life that you will not have even suspected only a few days ago. To a great extent you are keeping matters on the boil yourself because you are now driven by your own inner desire for change.

## 8 FRIDAY  ☿  *Moon Age Day 28  Moon Sign Sagittarius*

Restless and somewhat confused, the zodiac sign of Pisces needs time for reflection – but certainly not too much. There comes a moment when decisions have to be made and if you can't make up your own mind it might be useful to ask for an unbiased opinion from someone you really trust.

## 9 SATURDAY  ☿  *Moon Age Day 0  Moon Sign Capricorn*

Professional aims and objectives might be out of the window on a Saturday and so it is just as well that planetary trends right now favour a more relaxed approach to life, together with stronger social instincts. New friends are possible, together with a replay of a relationship from some time ago.

## 10 SUNDAY  ☿  *Moon Age Day 1  Moon Sign Capricorn*

What a good time this would be to start a completely new project. It probably won't be anything major and the implications are not earth shattering but it is important all the same. Your intellectual curiosity is stimulated and there is more than a little of the detective about you under present astrological trends.

## 11 MONDAY  ☿  *Moon Age Day 2  Moon Sign Aquarius*

Keep a sense of proportion regarding a difficult family issue. Any difficulties that come your way at the moment are likely to be the result of actions taken by others and you won't be quite as inspirational in your approach to the solutions as you were a few days ago. A little meditation might help.

## 12 TUESDAY  ☿  *Moon Age Day 3  Moon Sign Aquarius*

You are keen to take on any challenge that comes along at the moment and you have what it takes to get through obstacles that may have proved too much for you even yesterday. Try not to achieve too much all at once but use that natural patience of yours to get to your objectives sensibly and steadily.

## 13 WEDNESDAY ☿      *Moon Age Day 4    Moon Sign Pisces*

This is the time of the lunar high, the two or three-day period each month during which the Moon moves into your own zodiac sign of Pisces. You know what you want and how to get it, and you are keen to communicate this to others and inspire them with your enthusiasm. This is a time to shine.

## 14 THURSDAY ☿      *Moon Age Day 5    Moon Sign Pisces*

It isn't the details of life that interest you at the moment but rather the sort of over-view that allows you to make ground quickly. You won't be short of some important ideas and neither will you falter when you have to make quick decisions. Keep an open mind regarding emotional and romantic issues.

## 15 FRIDAY ☿      *Moon Age Day 6    Moon Sign Pisces*

Those who are in positions of authority are likely to be favourably disposed towards you at present and you can make the most of this situation by seeking something that is important to you. Having friends in high places is no bad thing and it isn't in the least selfish to want to get on in life.

## 16 SATURDAY ☿      *Moon Age Day 7    Moon Sign Aries*

Avoid getting bogged down by problems that are not of your making and which have little or nothing to do with you. Follow your own ideas and incentives and show some caution when others are putting you under any pressure. You are nobody's fool at the moment and won't be easily duped.

## 17 SUNDAY ☿      *Moon Age Day 8    Moon Sign Aries*

Even though Pisces is not the most outgoing of all the zodiac signs there won't be any chance to stand in the wings at present. People push you to the front and they will expect you to put on a good performance. This sort of thing is good for you because you are usually at your best when under just a little pressure.

## 18 MONDAY ☿      *Moon Age Day 9    Moon Sign Taurus*

In some way you are coming to the end of a long and somewhat awkward period, even if you don't entirely realise it at the moment. There are new starts ahead and you may get the chance to display some skills that even you didn't know you had. Throw caution to the wind in your social life this week.

## 19 TUESDAY ☿ *Moon Age Day 10   Moon Sign Taurus*

Intimate relationships should be working well today and you should be able to get close to someone who might have been difficult to approach of late. You have boundless energy at the moment, and some of this could be used to chase possibilities that have had to remain just that until recently.

## 20 WEDNESDAY ☿ *Moon Age Day 11   Moon Sign Gemini*

Get together with friends once the cares of the day are dealt with and don't allow minor concerns to get in the way of having a good time. Things are looking good on the romantic front for many sons and daughters of Pisces and it appears that you will be positively shining when in enjoyable company.

## 21 THURSDAY ☿ *Moon Age Day 12   Moon Sign Gemini*

Don't dwell too much on the past, not only because this takes you away from looking at the present and the future but mainly because you have so much to attend to right now. Rules and regulations, even domestic ones, might get on your nerves and what you really need is a complete break from routine.

## 22 FRIDAY ☿ *Moon Age Day 13   Moon Sign Cancer*

Results could easily exceed expectations at the moment and you may even surprise yourself with your new-found abilities. You should be happy and cheerful, so much so that people are putting you at the top of the favourites list. Some casual acquaintances could soon become much more to you.

## 23 SATURDAY ☿ *Moon Age Day 14   Moon Sign Cancer*

This may turn out to be a fairly busy day but it is one during which you must recognise your intuition and use it to the best of your ability. Almost anyone you meet at the moment can have an important message to impart. It's simply a case of paying attention and turning your thinking instincts up a notch.

## 24 SUNDAY ☿ *Moon Age Day 15   Moon Sign Leo*

It looks as though you can now plan ahead with a good deal of confidence and since those around you are so very supportive, co-operative plans go well too. What a great day this would be to take a journey. It doesn't matter if you are crossing the world or simply going into town. It's the change of scene that counts.

## 25 MONDAY ☿ *Moon Age Day 16   Moon Sign Leo*

You should be well aware of the effect you are having on others because your current popularity will allow you to take a few liberties and to ask for particular favours. People who hold positions of authority should notice Pisceans who are presently in employment more and more favourably.

## 26 TUESDAY ☿ *Moon Age Day 17   Moon Sign Leo*

You are very imaginative today and able to turn your attention towards making those little changes that will prove to be so important later on. Many Pisceans prove to be quite ingenious and if you are one of them it will be easy to get two or more gains from taking a single action.

## 27 WEDNESDAY *Moon Age Day 18   Moon Sign Virgo*

Things generally are likely to slow down for a day or two and there isn't really anything you can do about the situation. The Moon has moved into your opposite zodiac sign bringing the lunar low, an event that happens on a monthly cycle. Go with the flow and don't try to achieve too much.

## 28 THURSDAY *Moon Age Day 19   Moon Sign Virgo*

It is possible that the lunar low makes this another lacklustre day but much depends on your attitude and also on your aspirations. If you don't push too hard to achieve your objectives, you won't be disappointed when you can't achieve them. This is a time to stand on the riverbank of life and watch the water flow for a few hours.

## 29 FRIDAY *Moon Age Day 20   Moon Sign Libra*

Look for a time of renewed optimism and a period during which you should be getting on especially well in your career. Those of you who are between jobs at the moment need to keep your eyes wide open because offers could be coming along. All in all, you seem to be riding an important wave at the moment.

## 30 SATURDAY *Moon Age Day 21   Moon Sign Libra*

Someone could be challenging your views at this time and you need to be ready to defend a point of view you see as being valid. Attitude is very important when it comes to matters of the heart and this is no time to be hesitant or to stutter over words of love. Take a deep breath and say what you think.

## 31 SUNDAY
*Moon Age Day 22    Moon Sign Libra*

An exchange of views with even casual acquaintances could prove to be fun today and you will want to do everything you can to pep up the weekend with interesting activities. Many of you will be in the mood for shopping and it is likely you will be on the receiving end of a bargain.

# February

## 2016

## YOUR MONTH AT A GLANCE

(+) = Opportunities are around    (−) = Be on the defensive    = Life is pretty ordinary

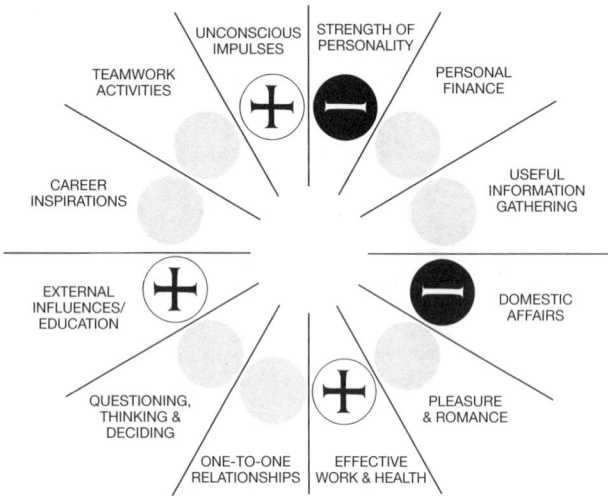

- UNCONSCIOUS IMPULSES (+)
- STRENGTH OF PERSONALITY (−)
- TEAMWORK ACTIVITIES
- PERSONAL FINANCE
- CAREER INSPIRATIONS
- USEFUL INFORMATION GATHERING
- EXTERNAL INFLUENCES/ EDUCATION (+)
- DOMESTIC AFFAIRS (−)
- QUESTIONING, THINKING & DECIDING
- PLEASURE & ROMANCE (+)
- ONE-TO-ONE RELATIONSHIPS
- EFFECTIVE WORK & HEALTH

## FEBRUARY HIGHS AND LOWS

*Here I show you how the rhythms of the Moon will affect you this month. Like the tide, your energies and abilities will rise and fall with its pattern. When it is above the centre line, go for it, when it is below, you should be resting.*

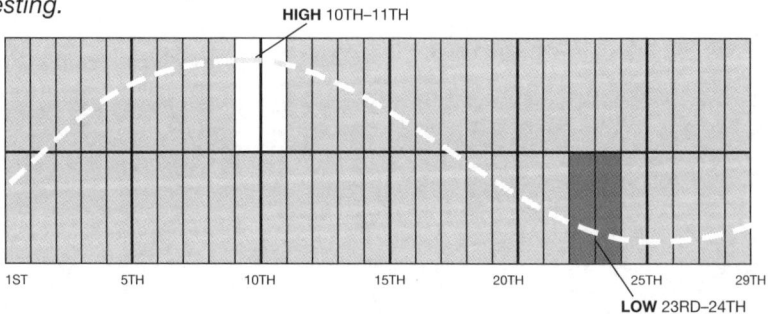

**HIGH** 10TH–11TH

1ST   5TH   10TH   15TH   20TH   25TH   29TH

**LOW** 23RD–24TH

## 1 MONDAY
*Moon Age Day 23    Moon Sign Scorpio*

The question arises today as to whether you want to continue in the direction you have previously chosen or change your mind. There is nothing at all wrong with modifying your opinions, even if you have to explain this to someone else. Keep a look out for some small financial gains around this time.

## 2 TUESDAY
*Moon Age Day 24    Moon Sign Scorpio*

Fulfil your need for variety and stimulation in just about any way you can today. If it is possible to take the day off work then so much the better. You are good company and great to be around generally. If there any frustrations at all today, these come from the direction of people who simply won't adapt.

## 3 WEDNESDAY
*Moon Age Day 25    Moon Sign Sagittarius*

You are now involved in a period of major change, some of which you haven't even chosen yourself. Having to constantly adapt isn't necessarily easy for your zodiac sign but it is very important. If you can manage to shrug your shoulders and simply watch what is happening around you, so much the better.

## 4 THURSDAY
*Moon Age Day 26    Moon Sign Sagittarius*

Apart from good trends in personal finances, this may be a rewarding time for renewing aspects of your personal life. You won't be making too many mistakes, either at work or at home and you should find yourself surrounded by people who quite obviously like you.

## 5 FRIDAY
*Moon Age Day 27    Moon Sign Sagittarius*

Your talent for understanding others has rarely been better than you find it at the moment. This would therefore be a good time to sort out the problems of a friend or even a family member. If you need to take advice from someone, you should turn to a wise old pal. They may not want you to reciprocate, though.

## 6 SATURDAY
*Moon Age Day 28    Moon Sign Capricorn*

Pisceans naturally seek out wisdom in all its forms, a search that can lead to many journeys and a good deal of study. You may find yourself in a state of intellectual curiosity today. There is much that is unusual about this part of February but it does make sense in a peculiar sort of way.

## 7 SUNDAY

Trends suggest that many of your thoughts are fleeting now but the intellectual activity that creates them is endless. You are at your happiest today when you are able to put your versatility to good use. New and positive beginnings are possible, not least in existing and new friendships.

## 8 MONDAY

You survive best in a secure family environment, with people around you who you know and trust. There are exceptions to this rule, a few of which may have been obvious recently. Your confidence remains generally high but there could be more than a little confusion in your mind.

## 9 TUESDAY

Your partner or someone else with whom you live might be on a very short fuse today. Since little or nothing can be gained from allowing yourself to become annoyed, it would be best to retreat from the situation. Behaving in this manner can be a Piscean fault but for now it is probably necessary.

## 10 WEDNESDAY

**Now is a period for putting new initiatives to the test and for getting on extremely well in life generally. In a social sense it is clear that you are sparkling like the morning sun, which offers all sorts of possibilities. You can afford to push your luck a little and should expect to make gains.**

## 11 THURSDAY

**There is great room for using your intuition and your practical skills this Thursday. Although someone is more or less bound to feel left out, it is imperative that you follow your own mind, no matter where it takes you. The slower types will simply have to catch up when they can.**

## 12 FRIDAY

Learning experiences remain pleasurable and offer you the chance to see yourself in a very different light. It might occur to you around now that much of what has been happening recently has had a very selfish aspect to it. This could be true but even your caring zodiac sign is allowed to be selfish sometimes.

## 13 SATURDAY
*Moon Age Day 5    Moon Sign Aries*

Personal relationships may be somewhat more troublesome than has been the case of late. Your partner could prove to be emotionally demanding and you won't have all the answers to the problems that family members are posing. Part of the reason for this is your slightly downbeat attitude today.

## 14 SUNDAY
*Moon Age Day 6    Moon Sign Taurus*

The desire for personal transformation continues, probably to a greater extent than has been the case for a number of months. Once the sign of Pisces gets itself into this frame of mind just about everyone takes notice. Although you are so keen to make alterations, do so by consensus and not argument.

## 15 MONDAY
*Moon Age Day 7    Moon Sign Taurus*

In discussions with partners, either personal or business ones, you need to be aware that you may not be making the sense you had hoped for. Practice what you have to say in front of a mirror and then ask yourself if your performance is good enough. If the answer is no, leave things until later.

## 16 TUESDAY
*Moon Age Day 8    Moon Sign Gemini*

Part of what you excel at right now is looking after other people. There is nothing in the least unusual about this for a Pisces subject but you are inclined to be extra attentive at the moment. Almost everyone you meet will respond to your natural kindness and easy-going attitude.

## 17 WEDNESDAY
*Moon Age Day 9    Moon Sign Gemini*

Don't believe everything you hear today because if you do there is just a chance you could be duped by someone. The best way to avoid this is to use your intuition, which is as strong as that possessed by any zodiac sign. Routines bring their own satisfaction now and you keep going when others get bored.

## 18 THURSDAY
*Moon Age Day 10    Moon Sign Cancer*

Not all of your responses appear to be very practical at the moment but the fact is that you see deep to the heart of situations and will be using some very original ways of sorting things out. Friends warm to you and will be more than willing to confide in you – sometimes in ways that could be surprising.

## 19 FRIDAY
*Moon Age Day 11    Moon Sign Cancer*

Spend at least part of today doing something that just pleases you. So much of your life is given over to helping others that you sometimes fail to address issues that are specifically important to your own life. You will revel in interesting company this Friday and can be the life and soul of social situations.

## 20 SATURDAY
*Moon Age Day 12    Moon Sign Cancer*

There is little slowing of the generally hectic lifestyle you are presently adopting and it is likely that new responsibilities fall upon your shoulders around now. These don't come like a bolt from the blue but are present because you show yourself to be so capable that others cannot fail to notice the fact.

## 21 SUNDAY
*Moon Age Day 13    Moon Sign Leo*

Don't force your opinions on to others and avoid appearing to know everything. It isn't often that Pisces appears in any way arrogant but that is the way you could come across just at the moment. People are so used to your natural humility that an over-confident Piscean is a real shocker.

## 22 MONDAY
*Moon Age Day 14    Moon Sign Leo*

Creature comforts are very important to you at the moment and that's not surprising during what is often one of the coldest and least inviting months of the year. You are only likely to come out of your shell if you feel anyone you care for is being threatened or if certain individuals are being unfair.

## 23 TUESDAY
*Moon Age Day 15    Moon Sign Virgo*

Things are quieter today and tomorrow and there appears to be very little you can do about the situation. You can thank the lunar low for the present state of affairs and should simply jog along as best you can. There may be some light relief coming from the comical behaviour of family members.

## 24 WEDNESDAY
*Moon Age Day 16    Moon Sign Virgo*

As long as you keep your hopes and dreams realistic, there is really no reason why today should work against you. Of course, it's going to be slow going but that is hardly likely to bother you all that much. What matters is the big picture and that looks as bright and hopeful as ever.

## 25 THURSDAY
*Moon Age Day 17    Moon Sign Libra*

Along comes a period of much stronger personal magnetism – so much so that your romantic life should be much more interesting. Friends should be warm and very attentive and you are likely to be feeling as contented as has been the case since the very start of this year.

## 26 FRIDAY
*Moon Age Day 18    Moon Sign Libra*

You could be in for a real red-letter day when it comes to information that will be of use to you in the near future. Avoid getting involved in family arguments or spats with friends that are of no real use. When others refuse to see eye-to-eye, you are the person who turns out to be the most reasonable.

## 27 SATURDAY
*Moon Age Day 19    Moon Sign Libra*

The trends for the weekend are definitely mixed and you tend to split your time between social events and the requirements of home. What really shines out at the moment is your sincerity and there isn't any doubt that people will trust you now with their innermost secrets.

## 28 SUNDAY
*Moon Age Day 20    Moon Sign Scorpio*

Challenges come along on a practical level but you will take these in your stride and won't be easily put off once you have made up your mind to a particular course of action. Sunday will be quieter than of late so you need to make as much movement as you can and do so as a deliberate strategy.

## 29 MONDAY
*Moon Age Day 21    Moon Sign Scorpio*

You continue to be a confidante for friends and relatives alike. So much honesty can sometimes be slightly difficult to take and you may need to spend just a little time alone in order to absorb all the information. However, you also show strong social inclinations and may decide a night out is in order.

# March

2016

## Your Month at a Glance

(+) = Opportunities are around      ⊖ = Be on the defensive      = Life is pretty ordinary

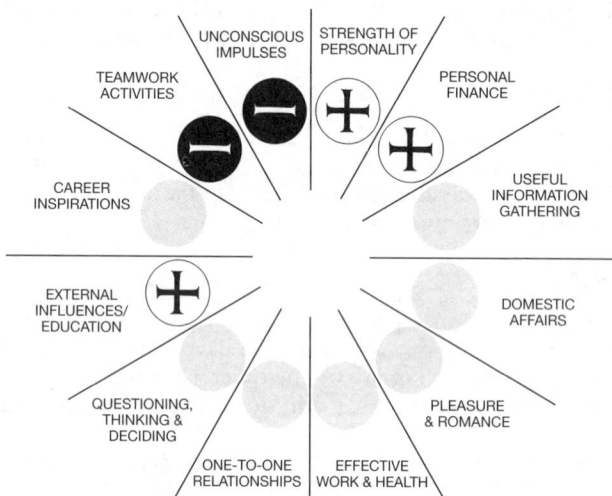

UNCONSCIOUS IMPULSES

STRENGTH OF PERSONALITY

TEAMWORK ACTIVITIES

PERSONAL FINANCE

CAREER INSPIRATIONS

USEFUL INFORMATION GATHERING

EXTERNAL INFLUENCES/ EDUCATION

DOMESTIC AFFAIRS

QUESTIONING, THINKING & DECIDING

PLEASURE & ROMANCE

ONE-TO-ONE RELATIONSHIPS

EFFECTIVE WORK & HEALTH

## March Highs and Lows

*Here I show you how the rhythms of the Moon will affect you this month. Like the tide, your energies and abilities will rise and fall with its pattern. When it is above the centre line, go for it, when it is below, you should be resting.*

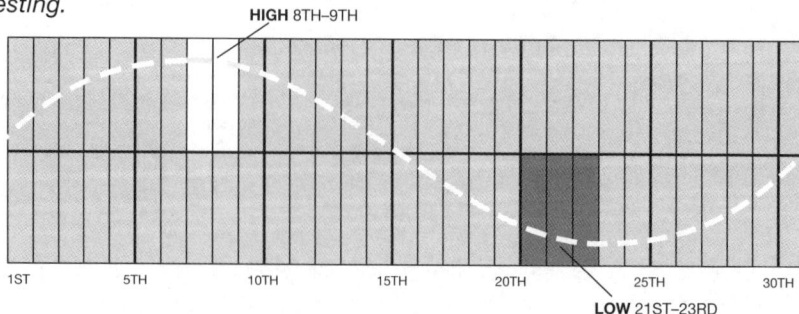

HIGH 8TH–9TH

1ST      5TH      10TH      15TH      20TH      25TH      30TH

LOW 21ST–23RD

## 1 TUESDAY
*Moon Age Day 22    Moon Sign Sagittarius*

You have good ideas for making money now and will be doing everything you can to show those around you how capable you are. With great vigour and a willingness to co-operate, this could turn out to be one of the best days of the month in a general sense. Friends should prove to be very interesting.

## 2 WEDNESDAY
*Moon Age Day 23    Moon Sign Sagittarius*

Trends suggest that there will be greater intimacy and romance around today. You have been busy with the practical side of life and may not have found the time to say the important things to those you love. Personal attachments take centre stage today and you will enjoy spending time with family members.

## 3 THURSDAY
*Moon Age Day 24    Moon Sign Sagittarius*

Beware of people who tell you that they know how you can get rich quick. For one thing they probably don't, and for another it would be quite easy for you to be conned at present. Big-time spending is out for the time being and you should keep a careful eye on your finances all round.

## 4 FRIDAY
*Moon Age Day 25    Moon Sign Capricorn*

Avoid dwelling too much on personal issues at the moment and don't worry if you are a little quieter than usual today. This often happens for a couple of days ahead of the lunar high and is quite natural. Today might offer new starts at work or at the very least different ways of looking at old matters.

## 5 SATURDAY
*Moon Age Day 26    Moon Sign Capricorn*

You have a wonderfully intuitive understanding of those around you. This isn't restricted to your partner or family members but extends to the world at large. The quality of your life is likely to be good right now and you show a cheerful face to the world, which is reflected back at you time and again.

## 6 SUNDAY
*Moon Age Day 27    Moon Sign Aquarius*

You cannot fail to make a positive impression on others today and should turn your mind towards having fun as part of a group. You might also be faced with the possibility of travel but are likely to be content to let others make the arrangements. There may also be room for changes within your home.

## 7 MONDAY
*Moon Age Day 28    Moon Sign Aquarius*

Today marks the start of a busy period when you will have less time than usual to relax. That won't bother you because you have a lot of energy. Almost everything you put your mind to works out the way you would wish, which is why this is a good time to make new starts and show your versatility.

## 8 TUESDAY
*Moon Age Day 0    Moon Sign Pisces*

**Plan something ambitious and push forward with all guns blazing. Trends suggest that you may be lucky at the moment, so you can afford to take a few small chances. Confidences come from all sorts of directions and you could learn something today that will shock and surprise you, though in a positive way.**

## 9 WEDNESDAY
*Moon Age Day 1    Moon Sign Pisces*

**You could feel frustrated if you are too quick on the uptake and expect more from people and situations than is reasonable. That famous Piscean patience is not much in evidence and you will need to work hard to keep your temper if you think you are being messed about. Avoid crowded places if you can.**

## 10 THURSDAY
*Moon Age Day 2    Moon Sign Aries*

Daily tasks can seem like much more of a chore than usual today, which is why you need to ring the changes whenever possible. The more widespread your interests, the greater is the chance that you will please yourself and others too. Some family pressures are likely but you may well shrug them off.

## 11 FRIDAY
*Moon Age Day 3    Moon Sign Aries*

Your expansive outlook and your tolerance make this an excellent time to be mixing freely, especially at work. You are probably capable of better things than those you are involved with right now and if you make sure you are in touch with the right people, improvements are quite possible.

## 12 SATURDAY
*Moon Age Day 4    Moon Sign Taurus*

In career matters you may now feel prepared to throw caution to the wind, which of course is fine if you happen to work at the weekend. From a social point of view you get along well with all sorts of people, whilst at the same time you may discover that a good deal of romantic attention is coming your way.

## 13 SUNDAY
*Moon Age Day 5    Moon Sign Taurus*

The major focus today is quite clearly on social matters, group interests and having fun. You show the very best of yourself in all situations that put you in the company of others and certainly should not be hiding your light under a bushel at the moment. Look for the odd or the unusual in life.

## 14 MONDAY
*Moon Age Day 6    Moon Sign Gemini*

Present astrological influences still favour good professional trends and bring you face-to-face with some long-standing ambitions. If you want to make the very best of yourself you will have to kill that slight shyness that is inherent in Pisces. Once you are into the swing of things you are anything but shy.

## 15 TUESDAY
*Moon Age Day 7    Moon Sign Gemini*

You are likely to spend more time helping others today than you will in thinking about your own life. It's possible that an old haunt comes into your mind and if you have the chance you may want to take a trip back in time. Although this can sometimes be disappointing, this isn't likely to be the case today.

## 16 WEDNESDAY
*Moon Age Day 8    Moon Sign Gemini*

The pace of life continues to be fairly brisk, even if there are moments today when you are not so sure of your direction. There are going to people around now who can help you decide about certain issues and although you have to make up your own mind in the end they will be able to assist you in the process.

## 17 THURSDAY
*Moon Age Day 9    Moon Sign Cancer*

You show desire to improve yourself in some way but although this is a very positive thing, it can be taken too far. There are certain aspects of your life that are quite all right as they are – no matter what other people may say. Don't allow yourself to be bullied into something that goes against the grain.

## 18 FRIDAY
*Moon Age Day 10    Moon Sign Cancer*

Life continues to go well in the main, though family concerns could creep in to spoil things just a little. Some of your worries are likely to prove groundless, and it is true that you sometimes have a tendency to worry unduly. Talking to friends will be especially helpful at the moment, particularly old, trusted pals.

## 19 SATURDAY
*Moon Age Day 11    Moon Sign Leo*

There are likely to be a great many strong opinions around at the moment, so adding your own to the pile probably won't help in most situations. You are an especially good listener at the moment and with just a few gentle words at the end of someone's tirade you could change their mind in a moment.

## 20 SUNDAY
*Moon Age Day 12    Moon Sign Leo*

With a strong emphasis in your chart now on work and productivity you may be able to see off most of your adversaries and competitors. This is not achieved through arguments or bluster, but rather through productive work. Happily, it will not be difficult to find some good allies.

## 21 MONDAY
*Moon Age Day 13    Moon Sign Virgo*

The monthly lull patch is now upon you so don't expect to make massive progress today or tomorrow. Concentrate on what is important and leave the dross until another time. Who knows, by the time you actually get round to doing those jobs you don't care for, someone else may have done them for you.

## 22 TUESDAY
*Moon Age Day 14    Moon Sign Virgo*

Some Pisceans may feel they are carrying the weight of the world around on their shoulders today. Of course this isn't the case and it is merely caused by the lunar low, which will soon be out of the way. Others may think you a little dramatic right now – which can be a fault of your Water-ruled zodiac sign.

## 23 WEDNESDAY
*Moon Age Day 15    Moon Sign Virgo*

People you haven't seen frequently in the recent past – or not at all – are likely to make a visit to your life, probably today. How you greet them depends on the nature of your last parting but if there is someone around with whom you have fallen out at some stage the time is now right to bury the hatchet.

## 24 THURSDAY
*Moon Age Day 16    Moon Sign Libra*

Make the most of what is being offered by close partnerships. The strongest planetary markers suggest that these will be romantic attachments, but there are also grounds for thinking that a new business partnership made at this time could go on to be not only satisfying but also very successful.

## 25 FRIDAY
*Moon Age Day 17    Moon Sign Libra*

It may not be easy to get along with those in authority today, although this may have more to do with the behaviour of others than with your own abilities. Use a little psychology and also turn your intuition up to full power. Nobody is better at assessing the way to approach others than you are.

## 26 SATURDAY
*Moon Age Day 18    Moon Sign Scorpio*

Stay away from personal conflict by refusing to allow discussions to turn into an argument. As the saying goes it takes two to tango and if you refuse to dance, peace and quiet will be the result. All the same, there are some antagonistic types around so be prepared to use your natural patience.

## 27 SUNDAY
*Moon Age Day 19    Moon Sign Scorpio*

Although you may not approach all social situations enthusiastically, you should not have a problem when you are mixing with people you know and like. You may be unnerved at present if you are surrounded by people you find intimidating or critical. As you need to feel comfortable today, stay away from such types if you possibly can.

## 28 MONDAY
*Moon Age Day 20    Moon Sign Scorpio*

This could be the start of one of the most romantic weeks of your year – but much depends on your own point of view and actions. It is likely to be Pisceans who are between relationships who get the most benefit from these trends but all Pisceans should receive significant attention and compliments.

## 29 TUESDAY
*Moon Age Day 21    Moon Sign Sagittarius*

Your natural curiosity is raised to fever pitch at the moment so it's little wonder you are making yourself party to any gossip that is going on in your vicinity. There isn't a situation around you that fails to arouse your interest and you will be looking in every crevice to seek the answers you know are there somewhere.

## 30 WEDNESDAY
*Moon Age Day 22    Moon Sign Sagittarius*

Your opinions could get you into a little trouble at the moment. You cannot pretend to hold a particular point of view when in reality you believe something quite different. All the same there are ways to be tactful and a Pisces subject understands these better than most. Some diplomacy is definitely called for.

# 31 THURSDAY
*Moon Age Day 23    Moon Sign Capricorn*

Make changes whilst the opportunity to do so is clear and defined. You won't achieve anything now by allowing situations to stand still and, in any case, the expectations others have of you demand action. Although you don't feel particularly lucky at present most of what you undertake should turn out well.

# April

2016

## Your Month at a Glance

(+) = Opportunities are around    ⊖ = Be on the defensive    = Life is pretty ordinary

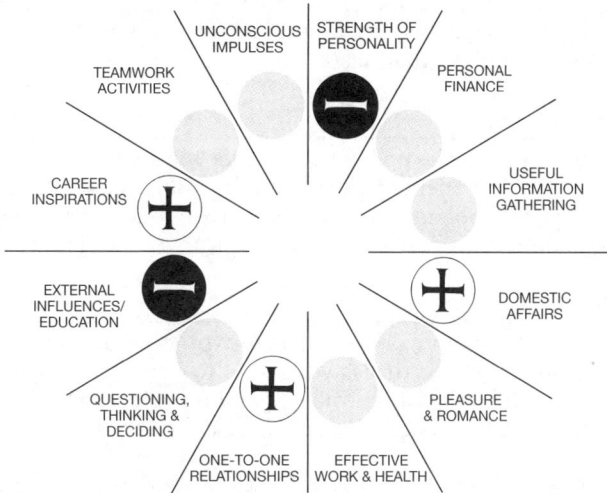

UNCONSCIOUS IMPULSES

STRENGTH OF PERSONALITY

TEAMWORK ACTIVITIES

PERSONAL FINANCE

CAREER INSPIRATIONS

USEFUL INFORMATION GATHERING

EXTERNAL INFLUENCES/ EDUCATION

DOMESTIC AFFAIRS

QUESTIONING, THINKING & DECIDING

PLEASURE & ROMANCE

ONE-TO-ONE RELATIONSHIPS

EFFECTIVE WORK & HEALTH

## April Highs and Lows

*Here I show you how the rhythms of the Moon will affect you this month. Like the tide, your energies and abilities will rise and fall with its pattern. When it is above the centre line, go for it, when it is below, you should be resting.*

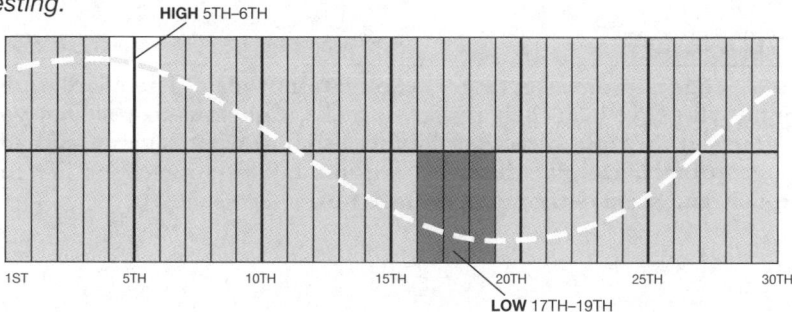

**HIGH** 5TH–6TH

1ST  5TH  10TH  15TH  20TH  25TH  30TH

**LOW** 17TH–19TH

## 1 FRIDAY
*Moon Age Day 24    Moon Sign Capricorn*

There are likely to be a few stresses in emotional attachments at the moment. The best way to avoid these is to keep things light and open. Deep and meaningful conversations are probably not the best way to move forward. On a different note, there could be slightly more cash about today than expected!

## 2 SATURDAY
*Moon Age Day 25    Moon Sign Capricorn*

The things you hear now are useful in a general sense and allow you to assist the world at large. You may not have a massive bearing on society, even at a local level, but every little helps. Concern for others is always a part of what you are but rarely more so than seems to be the case now.

## 3 SUNDAY
*Moon Age Day 26    Moon Sign Aquarius*

Your personal influence has not been stronger for a while than it proves to be right now. You have energy to spare and it should seem as though all the things you have been looking for manage to come together at the same time. Avoid taking on too much work because it is clear you need space to breathe.

## 4 MONDAY
*Moon Age Day 27    Moon Sign Aquarius*

A word in the right ear can work wonders for you now and brings you closer to achieving some objective that is very close to your heart. Spread out the responsibilities of the day and be willing to allow others to take some of the strain. It's a fair exchange because you are making them laugh.

## 5 TUESDAY
*Moon Age Day 28    Moon Sign Pisces*

**Professional advancement comes along as a result of who rather than what you know. Keep your eyes open because there are opportunities now to impress specific people, some of whom may be in a position to help you out. Your approach to life is now less likely to be clouded by deep thinking.**

## 6 WEDNESDAY
*Moon Age Day 29    Moon Sign Pisces*

**Trends suggest some sort of consolidation today. There are those around who have it in their power to make it obvious to you that you are going in the right direction. Simply listen to what is being said and act accordingly. Despite this, you are not taking yourself or life too seriously and seem determined to have fun.**

## 7 THURSDAY
*Moon Age Day 0    Moon Sign Aries*

There is a genuine possibility that you can move up the professional ladder at some stage soon. Keep your eye on whatever target you have set yourself and don't be willing to keep doing something you know is beneath your abilities. Others will help you out but most likely only if you ask.

## 8 FRIDAY
*Moon Age Day 1    Moon Sign Aries*

Ask yourself if your relatives and friends are behaving in the way that they are because that is what they wish to do or whether you might be manipulating them in some way. The fact is that you won't be happy with any result if it occurs to you later that you have applied any form of pressure.

## 9 SATURDAY
*Moon Age Day 2    Moon Sign Taurus*

It is true that the ups and downs of everyday life continue but you are in a good position to deal with both rationally and with great common sense. If there are disputes around, it is up to you to pour oil on troubled water. Even undertaking jobs you dislike is not going to be at all difficult.

## 10 SUNDAY
*Moon Age Day 3    Moon Sign Taurus*

You could be in need of some special help in order to get out of a jam, even though it is one that owes nothing to your own decisions or past actions. If you explain yourself to the right people, there is every reason to believe they can reverse difficult situations. Much of life is a state of mind at present.

## 11 MONDAY
*Moon Age Day 4    Moon Sign Gemini*

A planetary boost affecting social matters ought to become obvious around now, together with a real determination on your part to show what you are worth. The beginning of this week offers unexpected opportunities and leads you to a better understanding of your position at work and within the family.

## 12 TUESDAY
*Moon Age Day 5    Moon Sign Gemini*

Social matters and teamwork situations are where you encounter your most rewarding moments at this stage of the week. Someone is filled with admiration regarding the way you have dealt with a specific issue and it looks as though you are going to be number one in their books.

## 13 WEDNESDAY *Moon Age Day 6    Moon Sign Cancer*

It has never been easier to look at life through the eyes of other people and this can prove to be a tremendous gift. Don't worry about the somewhat offhand attitude of a particular friend. They are going through a rather hard time and could be inclined to lash out at those they care for the most.

## 14 THURSDAY *Moon Age Day 7    Moon Sign Cancer*

The things that others say have a great bearing on the way you think today. Although you are not likely to become depressed at this time, you are inclined to dig deep inside that inquiring mind of yours. If this gives others the impression you are down in the dumps you will want to reassure them this is not the case.

## 15 FRIDAY *Moon Age Day 8    Moon Sign Leo*

Although there is no shortage of things to be done, because you are adopting a new attitude you should find things falling into place quite neatly. Personal relationships are now an issue but in a far more positive way than appears to have been the case during the last couple of weeks.

## 16 SATURDAY *Moon Age Day 9    Moon Sign Leo*

There is plenty in your life to keep you happy at the moment, in fact at times there could be rather too much. You may need to slow things down a little or at the very least force yourself to concentrate on what you see as being the most important considerations for the weekend. Friends prove their loyalty today.

## 17 SUNDAY *Moon Age Day 10    Moon Sign Virgo*

You show yourself to be a good listener today, which is a positive way to use the lunar low period. There is time to hear exactly what other people are thinking and to do what you can to sort out their worries. You will keep confidences strictly and in return most people trust you implicitly.

## 18 MONDAY *Moon Age Day 11    Moon Sign Virgo*

You can expect a day during which you can't make the headway that has been obvious of late. All you can do is to show a degree of patience and to take a well-earned rest along the way. Don't let small irritations hold you back. The Moon might be in your opposite sign but Pisceans can usually ride this.

# 19 TUESDAY
*Moon Age Day 12    Moon Sign Virgo*

It looks as though you are managing to strike a happy balance between your responsibilities and your personal needs. If ever there was a good time to mix business with pleasure, this is it. New partnerships and associations are formed and you have what it takes to solve a long-standing problem.

# 20 WEDNESDAY
*Moon Age Day 13    Moon Sign Libra*

You feel a great need for personal satisfaction today and that means you will be slightly less giving to others and more inclined to feather your own nest. Bearing in mind that Pisces devotes a lot of time to help people in all walks of life, there is nothing at all wrong with occasionally putting yourself first.

# 21 THURSDAY
*Moon Age Day 14    Moon Sign Libra*

Keep up your efforts not only to have a good time but also to push forward with some plans that have been on hold for a while. Beneath the surface you might be worrying about family concerns but take comfort from the fact that these fears may sort themselves out.

# 22 FRIDAY
*Moon Age Day 15    Moon Sign Libra*

Positive trends are on the way. The Sun is moving into your solar third house, bringing a communicative month and putting you in the middle of all the exciting events. For the moment you will be occupied with important but dull jobs and probably may not even register that tomorrow is the weekend.

# 23 SATURDAY ☿
*Moon Age Day 16    Moon Sign Scorpio*

Your social life may yield some significant rewards, especially if you are willing to try something that you might have avoided in the past. Pisces gradually develops more confidence and has significant courage when it comes to a challenge. Make sure you don't forget a birthday or anniversary around this time.

# 24 SUNDAY ☿
*Moon Age Day 17    Moon Sign Scorpio*

It is likely that arrangements will have to be altered at the last moment and a trip you could have planned might well turn out to have a very unexpected itinerary. Today is all about flexibility and compromise. Although there could be frustrations as a result there are also likely to be pleasant surprises.

## 25 MONDAY ☿ *Moon Age Day 18    Moon Sign Sagittarius*

If you decide to seek out some peace and quiet today you will be disappointed. Life is all about activity for the moment and although that might seem stressful, in the longer-term you should reap the rewards. There isn't going to be much time for family today but you may be able to reassure someone in need.

## 26 TUESDAY ☿ *Moon Age Day 19    Moon Sign Sagittarius*

Today brings a brighter and fresher feel to your life and with the Sun shining away in your solar third house you feel a desire to communicate with others. It doesn't really matter who you talk to because it's the contact that is important. Beware of being critical of your partner – a row could be the result.

## 27 WEDNESDAY ☿ *Moon Age Day 20    Moon Sign Capricorn*

The creative side of your personality is now on display and you are able to put new projects into action. The midweek period should offer much in the way of social diversion and you will have a strong desire to get out and about. You also tend to look for exciting company under present trends.

## 28 THURSDAY ☿ *Moon Age Day 21    Moon Sign Capricorn*

There are some very strong views about just now and at least some of them will be yours. You won't accept anything from others that you see as being wrong or ill advised and may be more outspoken today and tomorrow than at any other time during April. Your ability to get things right first time is now amazing.

## 29 FRIDAY ☿ *Moon Age Day 22    Moon Sign Capricorn*

An extra push across the next couple of days can mean a lot of work saved in the longer-term. It is worth putting in some extra effort right now, even if you sometimes feel that everything depends upon you. Even if you allow others to take the lead, you are likely to be unhappy with their efforts.

## 30 SATURDAY ☿ *Moon Age Day 23    Moon Sign Aquarius*

It isn't that you are unresponsive today, more that you are thinking things through. You may come across as being slightly dull or uninterested and that's something you ought to avoid. You are comfortable with routine, and unlikely to do anything at the moment that even resembles breaking the mould.

# May

2016

## Your Month at a Glance

(+) = Opportunities are around    ⊖ = Be on the defensive    ○ = Life is pretty ordinary

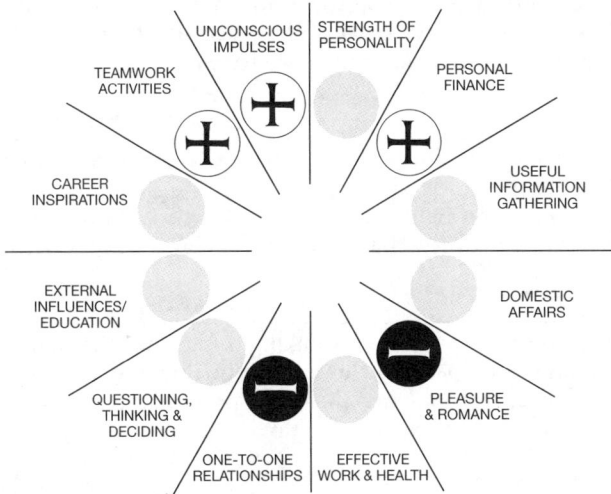

- UNCONSCIOUS IMPULSES
- STRENGTH OF PERSONALITY
- TEAMWORK ACTIVITIES
- PERSONAL FINANCE
- CAREER INSPIRATIONS
- USEFUL INFORMATION GATHERING
- EXTERNAL INFLUENCES/ EDUCATION
- DOMESTIC AFFAIRS
- QUESTIONING, THINKING & DECIDING
- PLEASURE & ROMANCE
- ONE-TO-ONE RELATIONSHIPS
- EFFECTIVE WORK & HEALTH

## May Highs and Lows

*Here I show you how the rhythms of the Moon will affect you this month. Like the tide, your energies and abilities will rise and fall with its pattern. When it is above the centre line, go for it, when it is below, you should be resting.*

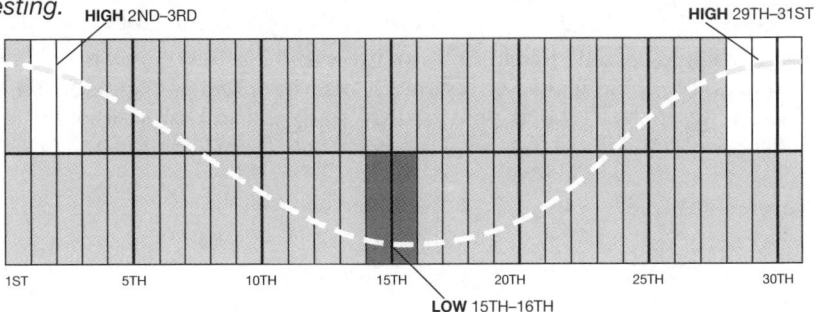

HIGH 2ND–3RD                                    HIGH 29TH–31ST

1ST    5TH    10TH    15TH    20TH    25TH    30TH

LOW 15TH–16TH

## 1 SUNDAY ☿ *Moon Age Day 24 Moon Sign Aquarius*

It is very important to make sure that you are properly in the know regarding things that are happening around you at the moment. Don't be too quick to jump to unnecessary conclusions, especially regarding the way others are behaving. Some small financial gains are also possible now.

## 2 MONDAY ☿ *Moon Age Day 25 Moon Sign Pisces*

**Now is the time to look out for a gift from Lady Luck, which shouldn't be hard to spot. Don't be afraid of some limited speculation, but make sure you use your intuition and common sense. Treat today as the beginning of a brighter and better phase because there are some potent planetary positions and aspects in store for you.**

## 3 TUESDAY ☿ *Moon Age Day 26 Moon Sign Pisces*

**Getting out and about should be easier now for two reasons: you have more time on your hands and also finances ought to be a little better than of late. Don't be held back by people who don't really have any better idea how to proceed than you have, even if they pretend they do.**

## 4 WEDNESDAY ☿ *Moon Age Day 27 Moon Sign Aries*

You can gain a great deal from simply talking things over today, partly because you are surrounded by people who are reasonable and who are willing to give you a fair hearing. At work there are potential gains in terms of the responsibilities you will be expected to take on in the future.

## 5 THURSDAY ☿ *Moon Age Day 28 Moon Sign Aries*

It is extremely important to you at the moment that you are liked. That's fine and it is part of the person you are but you can't expect everyone to think you are flavour of the month. Going to extremes to bring someone on-side who just doesn't understand the way you tick is a waste of energy.

## 6 FRIDAY ☿ *Moon Age Day 0 Moon Sign Taurus*

A total change of scene would suit you down to the ground now. Even if this is not possible you can at least ring the changes in one way or another. Those Pisceans who have decided on a holiday this early in the year could have made a very sensible decision. It is a break from routine you need the most.

## 7 SATURDAY ☿ *Moon Age Day 1    Moon Sign Taurus*

Your ability to communicate with your partner may not be so great at present, which is why help from a third party might prove to be necessary. All in all, this is not going to be a bad day but it could prove rather tedious unless you allow yourself the opportunity to break free from weekend routines in some way.

## 8 SUNDAY ☿ *Moon Age Day 2    Moon Sign Gemini*

Expect a slightly low-key sort of day and one during which you may not have quite the impact on the world you would wish. The more you commit yourself to routine matters, the less settled you could feel. Pisces is very thoughtful at present and it shows in most of what you do.

## 9 MONDAY ☿ *Moon Age Day 3    Moon Sign Gemini*

A sort of lively sociability seems to prevail as you embark on another working week. There probably won't be anything extraordinary about today but it does have its positive moments, not least in love. Explaining the way you feel about things right now brings you to a better understanding of yourself.

## 10 TUESDAY ☿ *Moon Age Day 4    Moon Sign Cancer*

Everyday routines keep you nicely on the go today, though you will find once again that there is probably very little to set this day apart and you may sometimes be a little bored with the routine elements of life. The answer lies in your own hands and is down to the amount of effort you choose to put in.

## 11 WEDNESDAY ☿ *Moon Age Day 5    Moon Sign Cancer*

Nobody doubts your natural charm or your ability to get on well with a range of different people. There are likely to be moments today in which you are going to be swept off your feet by the impact of another person. Take care, though, because this person's ability to influence you in the longer-term is suspect.

## 12 THURSDAY ☿ *Moon Age Day 6    Moon Sign Leo*

There is just a slight tendency for you to overcomplicate issues that are not really difficult at all. Try to remain on-track when it comes to your work, especially as you could be on the verge of advancement. Today is quite important as the planets suggest that others are watching your progress.

## 13 FRIDAY ☿        *Moon Age Day 7    Moon Sign Leo*

You are at the peak of your powers today, both mentally and probably physically. This might lead you on a fitness regime or down the road to other improvements you think are necessary. It would be sensible to plan such matters carefully because you show yourself as being slightly impulsive at present.

## 14 SATURDAY ☿      *Moon Age Day 8    Moon Sign Leo*

Your desire to escape is born of a number of different planetary positions and influences but since this is a Saturday, you could at least indulge yourself. It doesn't matter if you only go as far as your local shopping centre. What's important is that you don't lock yourself away at home this weekend.

## 15 SUNDAY ☿       *Moon Age Day 9    Moon Sign Virgo*

Despite the lunar low you should focus on practical matters, especially at work. Enlist the support of people you haven't been close to before and you might find you make one or two new friends. When you are free from work, you could find your mind wandering to some interesting and far-away places.

## 16 MONDAY ☿      *Moon Age Day 10    Moon Sign Virgo*

Today you should avoid being sidetracked by matters that are of no real importance. There is a danger that you could fall between two stools in the attitude you take towards specific issues, leaving you to doubt where your preferences really lie. In sporting activities, this is clearly a time to go for gold.

## 17 TUESDAY ☿      *Moon Age Day 11    Moon Sign Libra*

It's clear that you are now in the mood for excitement and in fact you can find it almost anywhere you go. Friends prove to be quite stimulating in their ideas and suggestions, whilst you may also discover hidden depths within colleagues. Don't get too hung up on doing the 'right thing' today but simply be yourself.

## 18 WEDNESDAY ☿      *Moon Age Day 12    Moon Sign Libra*

You may be surprised by events today and might have to react quickly if you want to benefit from instant opportunities. Nobody is in a better position to do so than you are and there are strong planetary influences indicating that success will arise as a result of the intervention of your friends.

## 19 THURSDAY ☿ *Moon Age Day 13   Moon Sign Libra*

Pisces now displays a real desire to break out of restrictive situations and with the advancing summer you will also be anxious to spend more time out of doors. All in all, this would be a fine time to plan a holiday at short notice or just take a couple of days away. Everyday routines may seem quite tedious.

## 20 FRIDAY ☿ *Moon Age Day 14   Moon Sign Scorpio*

You will remain keen to break out of long-established patterns, even though these can be quite comfortable on occasions. Any feelings of uneasiness are quite understandable because you rely heavily on the past and also on certain conventions. All the same change is necessary and once undertaken it benefits you.

## 21 SATURDAY ☿ *Moon Age Day 15   Moon Sign Scorpio*

This might be a good time to revitalise certain elements of your personal life and to find out exactly how your partner feels about life. In most respects you already know because you are a sensitive soul and always bear others in mind. However, there may be some things that people haven't been telling you.

## 22 SUNDAY ☿ *Moon Age Day 16   Moon Sign Sagittarius*

If you expect rewarding experiences today they are yours for the taking. Some of these may take place at home, or at least in the company of your family. Friends won't be taking a back seat, though, because it is likely that later in the day you will be socially active and happy to join in with anything.

## 23 MONDAY *Moon Age Day 17   Moon Sign Sagittarius*

There are people around at the moment who have everything it takes to irritate you. You may not be surprised by who is getting your goat but you do have what it takes to deal with them in a different way. Compromise – without surrendering what is really important to you – is the way forward.

## 24 TUESDAY *Moon Age Day 18   Moon Sign Sagittarius*

You may need to take time out in order to address a few practical issues, whilst at the same time getting on with the sort of jobs you would prefer to leave totally alone. Who knows? It might be possible to get others to lend a hand, and turn some irritating chores into a feast of fun. All you really have to do is ask.

## 25 WEDNESDAY
*Moon Age Day 19    Moon Sign Capricorn*

Using just your natural charm you can get almost anything you want today. It's true that your requirements are more modest than most but even you may decide that you deserve a little more right now. If there are any difficulties within personal and romantic attachments, talk things through carefully.

## 26 THURSDAY
*Moon Age Day 20    Moon Sign Capricorn*

Your personal involvement with co-workers may be quite crucial towards the end of this month, probably because they have something you need, whilst you possess knowledge that is vital to them. Successful, albeit short-term, partnerships could be the result. There are some unusual alliances to be formed.

## 27 FRIDAY
*Moon Age Day 21    Moon Sign Aquarius*

Do what you can to improve your lot socially – perhaps by mixing with a slightly different set of people and by showing your potential more readily. All you really have to do is to turn your charisma up a notch and then wait for the reaction. Your ability to influence people now is not in question.

## 28 SATURDAY
*Moon Age Day 22    Moon Sign Aquarius*

You can expect a few ups and downs within personal relationships today, which is why the wisest amongst you will be spending at least some of your spare time with friends. It might seem especially good to be with people whose emotional attachment to you isn't quite so deep and who want to be casual in their approach.

## 29 SUNDAY
*Moon Age Day 23    Moon Sign Pisces*

**The Moon sails majestically into your zodiac sign and brings with it a host of new possibilities. Not only are energy levels extremely high at the moment, you also have the genuine good luck necessary to get ahead. Don't allow people who barely know you to have a say in your behaviour.**

## 30 MONDAY
*Moon Age Day 24    Moon Sign Pisces*

**There has probably not been a potentially better day this month as far as you are concerned. Your judgement is good and you feel as though you could run the world single-handedly. Of course this isn't true but at least dealing with your small part of it ought to be child's play at the moment.**

## 31 TUESDAY

Ingenious ideas are around in abundance and all it requires is a little extra effort and courage from you in order to embrace them. Friends in particular have things to say that will set off your own imagination and lead you down different paths. This is likely to be a day that offers a lot in the way of excitement.

# June

2016

## Your Month at a Glance

(+) = Opportunities are around    (–) = Be on the defensive    = Life is pretty ordinary

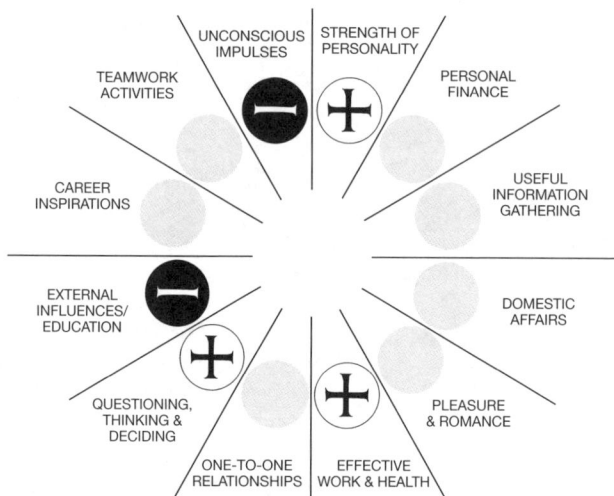

UNCONSCIOUS IMPULSES

STRENGTH OF PERSONALITY

TEAMWORK ACTIVITIES

PERSONAL FINANCE

CAREER INSPIRATIONS

USEFUL INFORMATION GATHERING

EXTERNAL INFLUENCES/ EDUCATION

DOMESTIC AFFAIRS

QUESTIONING, THINKING & DECIDING

PLEASURE & ROMANCE

ONE-TO-ONE RELATIONSHIPS

EFFECTIVE WORK & HEALTH

## June Highs and Lows

*Here I show you how the rhythms of the Moon will affect you this month. Like the tide, your energies and abilities will rise and fall with its pattern. When it is above the centre line, go for it, when it is below, you should be resting.*

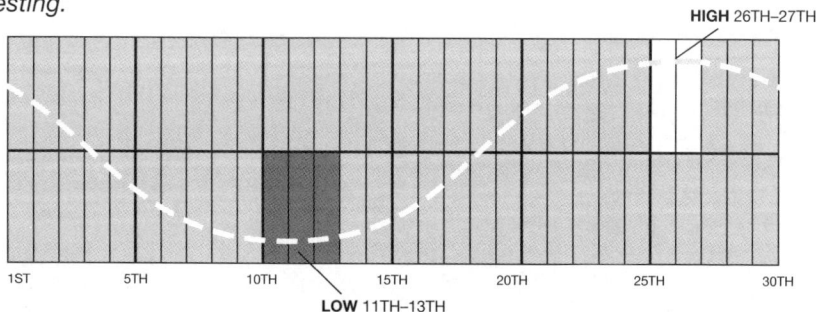

**HIGH** 26TH–27TH

1ST    5TH    10TH    15TH    20TH    25TH    30TH

**LOW** 11TH–13TH

## 1 WEDNESDAY

You need to work hard at what you like today because then you will improve your performance. Leave aside the jobs you don't care for, at least until tomorrow. Also, the more enjoyment you get into your life, the better you will get on with those around you. This ought to be a generally satisfying day.

## 2 THURSDAY

A more inward looking phase is at hand, though it probably won't last very long. You need to be introspective now and again and can gain as a result. If there is any problem at all it comes because those around you might think they have upset you in some way. Offer a little reassurance that this isn't the case.

## 3 FRIDAY

You don't mind working extra hard for some material benefits and there are plenty of them on offer when you look around. It seems you are now more likely to throw yourself into the maelstrom that is affecting certain aspects of your life and you have the ability to bring a degree of order out of apparent chaos.

## 4 SATURDAY

Focus your energies on the material side of life, even though you may instinctively want to stick to what is warm and personal. You have to be in the midst of things if you want to see success coming your way and, in any case, once you get started you will be glad of the good results that quickly arise.

## 5 SUNDAY

You may be forced to relinquish something in your personal life because it is obvious that changes are necessary. These may not relate directly to relationships but rather the circumstances that surround them. It is possible that someone in the background could be the source of the problem.

## 6 MONDAY

Getting out and about should bring you into contact with those you find stimulating, interesting and useful. This may not be a day during which you get a great deal done in a material sense but you can have fun and after a reasonably quiet period that's important. Your creative potential is also improved.

## 7 TUESDAY
*Moon Age Day 3    Moon Sign Cancer*

You can now look forward to some highlights in terms of friendship. Present trends are such that you will not only be getting on well with existing pals but probably making some new ones too. Don't get caught up in discussions or arguments that are not of your making and have nothing to do with you.

## 8 WEDNESDAY
*Moon Age Day 4    Moon Sign Cancer*

Getting together in group encounters suits you fine now. With offers on the table you could be planning something particularly exciting. For the moment you may have to catch up with one or two jobs but will be merely setting the scene for bigger and better things that are soon to come.

## 9 THURSDAY
*Moon Age Day 5    Moon Sign Leo*

Today there ought to be a brand new focus on fresh initiatives and you can't afford to stand around and wait for life to come to you. While things are so positive you should be out there getting what you want, even in the face of a little opposition. People will come round to your point of view in time.

## 10 FRIDAY
*Moon Age Day 6    Moon Sign Leo*

Avoid showing the possessive side of your nature, which does surface now and again. Any form of jealousy is simply a waste of time and effort and in any case you may be wrong in your assumptions. There are gains to be made today but you will have to look at matters closely to find them.

## 11 SATURDAY
*Moon Age Day 7    Moon Sign Virgo*

The lull patch brought about by the lunar low will probably have less of a bearing on your life this time round, though you will once again have to work hard to get what you want from life. Attitude is all-important when you are dealing with people who are positive and assertive but you can match them.

## 12 SUNDAY
*Moon Age Day 8    Moon Sign Virgo*

Today is likely to be another slightly quiet day but one that still offers a great deal if you are willing to go out and get it. You will need to plan carefully at the moment in order to make certain you don't become bogged down with details. The path ahead is far from clear but you make progress one step at a time.

## 13 MONDAY
*Moon Age Day 9    Moon Sign Virgo*

The planetary picture shows that your love life may be the one area through which you will have to tread somewhat carefully. People are very sensitive right now and that means it would be very easy to upset them. Avoid family arguments or any sort of dispute that you cannot hope to win.

## 14 TUESDAY
*Moon Age Day 10    Moon Sign Libra*

Take care when you are investing money or making decisions that are going to have a bearing on your life for some time to come. Advice is available when you need it but this relies upon you recognising it when it is offered. Try to see people you don't meet up with very often and simply enjoy their company.

## 15 WEDNESDAY
*Moon Age Day 11    Moon Sign Libra*

For much of the time co-operative ventures look particularly good and there isn't much to stand in your way when you are sharing jobs with those around you. Unfortunately, not everyone may feel like mucking in and you might have to deal with some fairly grumpy types too.

## 16 THURSDAY
*Moon Age Day 12    Moon Sign Scorpio*

It might be difficult for you to feel totally in charge of practical matters today and this could force you to seek help and advice from some rather odd directions. Fortunately your mind is open to curious associations and connections, which is a distinct advantage now. Ordinary routines may seem boring.

## 17 FRIDAY
*Moon Age Day 13    Moon Sign Scorpio*

Don't allow obligations to prevent you from making new achievements. It's fine to work on behalf of the world but you sometimes take things too far. In any case, if you are content and happy with your lot you will be in a better position to continue sorting out everyone else's lives. New experiences are necessary.

## 18 SATURDAY
*Moon Age Day 14    Moon Sign Scorpio*

There are times at the moment when the difficulties which arise from personal attachments seem more trouble than they are worth, though in your heart you know this is not the case. Just a little extra effort can sort things out but don't focus on these matters to the exclusion of all else today.

## 19 SUNDAY
*Moon Age Day 15   Moon Sign Sagittarius*

You are probably pushing on with certain aspects of your life much faster than expected. Things seem to fall into place easily, and what is more there is plenty of support coming from the direction of family members and friends. From a financial point of view you might be unexpectedly rather better off now.

## 20 MONDAY
*Moon Age Day 16   Moon Sign Sagittarius*

This ought to be an especially busy day for comings and goings – not just your own either because people you don't see too often could make an appearance in your life. Opt for the line of least resistance in things that are not too important because this leaves you more time and energy to concentrate on what really matters to you.

## 21 TUESDAY
*Moon Age Day 17   Moon Sign Capricorn*

Develop your own ambitions today and don't get too carried away with the ideas of other people. To have the courage of your own convictions does mean that if anything goes wrong you will take the blame. On the other hand you will also get all the accolades when they go well – which on the whole is far more likely.

## 22 WEDNESDAY
*Moon Age Day 18   Moon Sign Capricorn*

Don't be in too much of a rush to achieve all your objectives at the same time. You can afford to wait and allow things to mature in their own time. As you are from one of the most patient of all zodiac signs you should be happy to do this. Look at the wider picture at work and don't get hung up on details.

## 23 THURSDAY
*Moon Age Day 19   Moon Sign Aquarius*

If you approach matters with greater than usual compliance you could be swept into things that you would prefer to avoid. Under changing planetary trends it is actually quite important for you to stick to your guns on issues that are personally important to you. This is necessary – but not easy.

## 24 FRIDAY
*Moon Age Day 20   Moon Sign Aquarius*

Anything routine or boring is going to get on your nerves today and you will be at your very best when you are able to pursue your own desires as you wish. Part of the reason for this is that other people just don't have what it takes to keep up with you and you are insistent that things should be done your way.

## 25 SATURDAY
*Moon Age Day 21    Moon Sign Aquarius*

It is quite probable that you will be running around making last minute changes to any sort of arrangement today. This would be especially true in the case of Pisceans who are either going on holiday or simply taking a weekend break. In some respects it would be far less tiring to simply remain at home!

## 26 SUNDAY
*Moon Age Day 22    Moon Sign Pisces*

**There are great planetary trends around for Pisces and these are particularly significant ahead of another working week. With everything to play for and people taking so much notice of you, speak out for what you want. Nobody will accuse you of being selfish because your zodiac sign simply isn't made that way.**

## 27 MONDAY
*Moon Age Day 23    Moon Sign Pisces*

**The planets suggest that today you might get the opportunity to do your own thing. Practically everyone you come across is opening new doors for you and making it possible for you to shine. There might not be many huge practical gains today but the social ones more than make up for this.**

## 28 TUESDAY
*Moon Age Day 24    Moon Sign Aries*

Pleasant trends now surround romance and it is towards love that many Pisceans will be looking this particular day. Keep yourself in the best of company and avoid loud or vexatious types for the moment. The more serene your surroundings the better you will fare when it comes to thinking up words of love.

## 29 WEDNESDAY
*Moon Age Day 25    Moon Sign Aries*

Stand by for a very hectic period at home, even if things are much quieter as far as work is concerned. Your closest relatives simply demand your attention and since there is a great deal going on in their lives you will be more than happy to lend a hand. It looks as though a celebration is likely – a wedding perhaps?

## 30 THURSDAY
*Moon Age Day 26    Moon Sign Taurus*

Family matters bring the greatest rewards today and you could do far worse than to indulge in something that is designed to please you. Although you will fulfil your responsibilities out there in the wider world, it is when you are within your own four walls that you will feel most content. Money matters are variable now.

♓

# July

2016

## YOUR MONTH AT A GLANCE

⊕ = Opportunities are around     ⊖ = Be on the defensive     ○ = Life is pretty ordinary

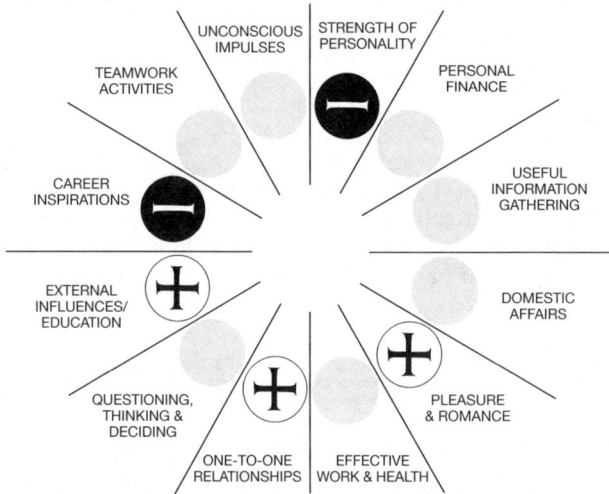

UNCONSCIOUS IMPULSES

STRENGTH OF PERSONALITY

TEAMWORK ACTIVITIES

PERSONAL FINANCE

CAREER INSPIRATIONS ⊖

USEFUL INFORMATION GATHERING

EXTERNAL INFLUENCES/ EDUCATION ⊕

DOMESTIC AFFAIRS

QUESTIONING, THINKING & DECIDING

⊕

PLEASURE & ROMANCE ⊕

ONE-TO-ONE RELATIONSHIPS

EFFECTIVE WORK & HEALTH

## JULY HIGHS AND LOWS

*Here I show you how the rhythms of the Moon will affect you this month. Like the tide, your energies and abilities will rise and fall with its pattern. When it is above the centre line, go for it, when it is below, you should be resting.*

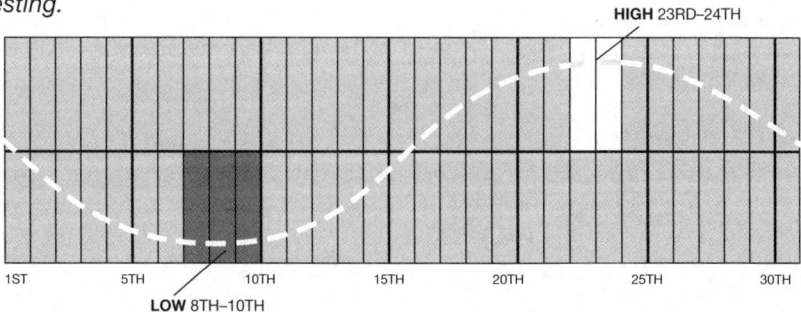

**HIGH** 23RD–24TH

| 1ST | 5TH | 10TH | 15TH | 20TH | 25TH | 30TH |

**LOW** 8TH–10TH

84

## 1 FRIDAY
*Moon Age Day 27    Moon Sign Taurus*

There are some gains to be made, especially later on today. Although may not feel yourself to have quite the incentive you might wish, it is only a matter of time before you begin to push forward progressively again. Finances take some careful looking at before you commit yourself to new expenditure.

## 2 SATURDAY
*Moon Age Day 28    Moon Sign Gemini*

Don't miss out on any important news that is going around at present. This is a very sociable Saturday and a time during which you will be happy to spend a few hours chewing the fat with those you know and like the best. Good fortune is likely to follow your footsteps across the next few days.

## 3 SUNDAY
*Moon Age Day 29    Moon Sign Gemini*

Getting what you want from others and from specific situations now appears to be much easier. The shy and retiring side of the sign of Pisces takes a definite holiday around now as you push forward with new incentives and with a confidence that others will find quite astonishing in your case.

## 4 MONDAY
*Moon Age Day 0    Moon Sign Cancer*

The pursuit of practical matters offers a greater chance of success than spending hours thinking things through. For a few Pisceans yesterday may have been time for consideration, whereas now is the moment to strike. There is certainly assistance around when you require it, though you might have to ask.

## 5 TUESDAY
*Moon Age Day 1    Moon Sign Cancer*

Your acquisitive streak is definitely on display and you also know full well how to make money this week. Although you are rarely obsessed with material things, you are likely to be so to a greater extent now. Acting on impulse seems attractive but might not pay too many dividends at present.

## 6 WEDNESDAY
*Moon Age Day 2    Moon Sign Leo*

If there is something or someone holding you back around this time, it would be sensible to try to sort it out. Don't focus on your perceived limitations, even though this is an inherent part of your Piscean nature – it won't get you very far at present. A new appraisal of old situations is called for.

## 7 THURSDAY
*Moon Age Day 3    Moon Sign Leo*

Daily life should have plenty to keep you both occupied and interested at this stage of a generally active week. Rules and regulations are easy to deal with – you will simply ignore them if they get in your way. Not everyone is going to be co-operative now so stick to those who are.

## 8 FRIDAY
*Moon Age Day 4    Moon Sign Virgo*

All of a sudden you experience some reversals of fortune. Don't react too strongly to these because they are only caused by the lunar low. In a couple of days you will be right back on form, so for the moment show some of that Piscean patience and be willing to wait in order to pursue your dreams.

## 9 SATURDAY
*Moon Age Day 5    Moon Sign Virgo*

An extra bit of effort really counts for a great deal at this time, which is why you are likely to be willing to march forward with determination, even though the lunar low can make this more difficult than usual. Be careful, though, because you might be expending more energy than is strictly necessary.

## 10 SUNDAY
*Moon Age Day 6    Moon Sign Virgo*

There are some promising financial developments about and you will want to make the most of them when you can. Keep an eye open for opportunities that mean new investments, although do bear in mind that you need to think in terms of the more distant future. Romance is well-starred today.

## 11 MONDAY
*Moon Age Day 7    Moon Sign Libra*

Don't begin new ventures, only to leave them hanging in the air. This is a time when you should concentrate on one thing at a time and get it done before you look elsewhere. If you scatter your energies and resources you will only find yourself repeating the same task over and over again.

## 12 TUESDAY
*Moon Age Day 8    Moon Sign Libra*

You can make great gains at work today, particularly as you are presently willing to take the sort of chances you would have shied away from only a short time ago. The attitude of your family and friends presently makes it that much easier to gain their trust and co-operation in all matters.

# 13 WEDNESDAY
*Moon Age Day 9   Moon Sign Scorpio*

There can be a strong sense of nostalgia around at this time, leading you to spend as much time today looking back as you do forward. This contrasts markedly with your desire to get ahead and so some conflict tends to crop up within your mind today. Resolve these issues by talking about them.

# 14 THURSDAY
*Moon Age Day 10   Moon Sign Scorpio*

You should feel energetic and strong, which is why you could be so adventurous at present. You may even be surprised at your own tenacity and bravery, leading you to little adventures you can really enjoy. Not everyone seems to be on your side at present, though the most important people will be.

# 15 FRIDAY
*Moon Age Day 11   Moon Sign Scorpio*

Half way through the month and you still haven't done some of the things that seemed important right back at the end of June. Now is the time to assess the way situations are unfolding and to offer that extra assistance that is going to be necessary to get new plans off the drawing board and into reality.

# 16 SATURDAY
*Moon Age Day 12   Moon Sign Sagittarius*

Your present winning ways lead to some high spots as far as your social life is concerned and you may also be wowing them in the aisles in terms of your romantic overtures. People like you and you revel in the attention that comes your way, even if you try to be modest and pretend you haven't noticed!

# 17 SUNDAY
*Moon Age Day 13   Moon Sign Sagittarius*

Your outlook at the moment is expansive, optimistic and generous – which is really the ideal of Pisces when working at its very best. Present trends favour travel, learning and cultural activities of almost any sort and assist you to get the most from life. It's a pity all your friends are not so sorted right now.

# 18 MONDAY
*Moon Age Day 14   Moon Sign Capricorn*

There's a chance that you will be fully absorbed in your career at the start of this week – or else totally committed to study if you are presently involved in education of any sort. This might not leave quite as much time for socialising as you would wish but your sense of commitment is the overriding factor.

## 19 TUESDAY
*Moon Age Day 15   Moon Sign Capricorn*

Romance is truly where it's at now for many sons and daughters of Pisces. You show yourself to be charming and entertaining company and will love to be the centre of attention. What is more, you have an innate ability to mix business with pleasure in such a way that you manage to keep everyone happy.

## 20 WEDNESDAY
*Moon Age Day 16   Moon Sign Capricorn*

Your energy levels remain generally high and your spirits are strong. You would be particularly good today when involved in any sort of sporting activity, or else situations that demand a great deal of thought allied to physical stamina. Although you are quite competitive at the moment your sensitivity will not suffer as a result.

## 21 THURSDAY
*Moon Age Day 17   Moon Sign Aquarius*

Some situations require compromise, a fact that you understand much better than most. Although you might have to give away more than you would wish today, the results are likely to justify your actions. Stay away from pointless gossip that pours ridicule or scorn on one individual. That's not your style at all.

## 22 FRIDAY
*Moon Age Day 18   Moon Sign Aquarius*

Today could be slightly slower than you might have wished or anticipated, mainly because you are simply not as energetic as before. This will change again tomorrow but for the moment you would be better off spending just a little time on your own and seeking moments when you can think things through quietly.

## 23 SATURDAY
*Moon Age Day 19   Moon Sign Pisces*

**It might be said that a little luck is on your side today but the simple fact is that you are making your own luck as you go along. Don't be afraid to show others what you are capable of achieving and be willing to share your new views regarding work with colleagues and bosses alike.**

## 24 SUNDAY
*Moon Age Day 20   Moon Sign Pisces*

**You should be able to make full use of all the opportunities that come your way at present. Most spheres of your life benefit from the presence of the lunar high but none more so than romance. Whether you have an established relationship or are just beginning a new one, today offers opportunities.**

## 25 MONDAY                    *Moon Age Day 21    Moon Sign Aries*

This is one of the best phases of the year for making money but there is more to life than cash and you are also very inclined to travel right now. Any opportunity to do both should be seized and it should be possible to achieve your financial goals whilst expanding your general horizons at the same time.

## 26 TUESDAY                   *Moon Age Day 22    Moon Sign Aries*

Success and progress in the workplace now seems more or less assured – if you take the right steps early in the day. If you falter right now it is likely to be because you haven't prepared yourself properly or because you are too reliant on the sort of advice you know to be unsound. Use your powers of reason.

## 27 WEDNESDAY                 *Moon Age Day 23    Moon Sign Taurus*

Almost any sort of partnership seems to be working out well for you at present and make the most of any chance you get to make a new alliance at work. Those Pisceans who are self-employed might be the luckiest of all right now because you may discover new ways to spread your message far and wide.

## 28 THURSDAY                  *Moon Age Day 24    Moon Sign Taurus*

Your strong perception and natural insight can see you through a couple of potentially difficult situations and there isn't any doubt right now about your ability to sort the wheat from the chaff. At work you should be showing just what you are capable of achieving and can prove your worth in a dozen different ways.

## 29 FRIDAY                    *Moon Age Day 25    Moon Sign Gemini*

The more you are amongst other people today the greater is the chance that you make a favourable impression. That might not matter too much just at the moment but you are laying down the path for gains in the future. Don't miss any opportunity to show everyone you meet just how capable you can be.

## 30 SATURDAY                  *Moon Age Day 26    Moon Sign Gemini*

When it comes to being thorough you seem to be in your element this weekend. No detail is left unnoticed and you have what it takes to see the smallest potential difficulties and sort them out in advance. Friends may marvel at your ability to pour oil on troubled waters and as a result you are now very popular.

# 31 SUNDAY

*Moon Age Day 27   Moon Sign Cancer*

Your ability to delegate is now one of your natural talents, and this really shows well under present planetary positions. What you seek the most at the moment is co-operation and you shouldn't have to work too hard to find it. People co-operate not because you intimidate them but because they like and respect you.

# August 2016

## YOUR MONTH AT A GLANCE

(+) = Opportunities are around     ⊖ = Be on the defensive     ○ = Life is pretty ordinary

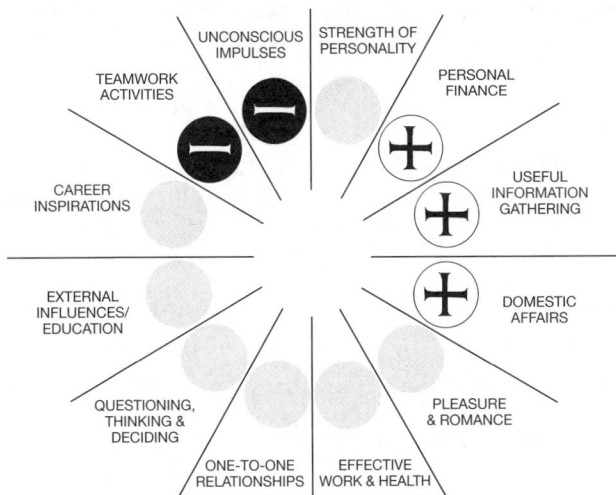

- UNCONSCIOUS IMPULSES ⊖
- STRENGTH OF PERSONALITY
- TEAMWORK ACTIVITIES ⊖
- PERSONAL FINANCE
- CAREER INSPIRATIONS
- USEFUL INFORMATION GATHERING (+)
- PERSONAL FINANCE (+)
- EXTERNAL INFLUENCES/ EDUCATION
- DOMESTIC AFFAIRS (+)
- QUESTIONING, THINKING & DECIDING
- PLEASURE & ROMANCE
- ONE-TO-ONE RELATIONSHIPS
- EFFECTIVE WORK & HEALTH

## AUGUST HIGHS AND LOWS

*Here I show you how the rhythms of the Moon will affect you this month. Like the tide, your energies and abilities will rise and fall with its pattern. When it is above the centre line, go for it, when it is below, you should be resting.*

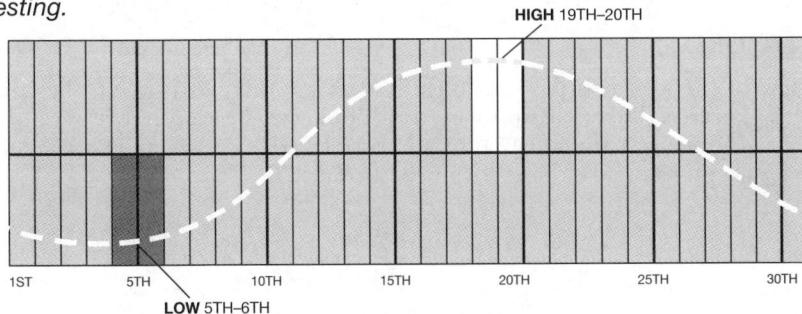

**HIGH** 19TH–20TH

1ST     5TH     10TH     15TH     20TH     25TH     30TH

**LOW** 5TH–6TH

## 1 MONDAY
*Moon Age Day 28    Moon Sign Cancer*

As you now find yourself motivated by material issues, you should be far more willing than usual to feather your own nest. Of course, being the sort of person you are, it will be necessary for you to prove to yourself that you are helping others on the way, but that's simply your caring side on display.

## 2 TUESDAY
*Moon Age Day 0    Moon Sign Cancer*

You are stimulated by meetings with new people at this time. As a result, you should be in for a distinctly social time and one that encourages gatherings with individuals you might have shied away from in the past. This is not a period when you are likely to make too many mistakes, no matter what you take on.

## 3 WEDNESDAY
*Moon Age Day 1    Moon Sign Leo*

You are likely to be filled with good ideas today and more than happy to put a few of them into practice. It appears that your ingenuity is really showing and this leads you to getting your own way, even via rather strange routes. Friends and relatives alike should be paying you a great deal of attention.

## 4 THURSDAY
*Moon Age Day 2    Moon Sign Leo*

You are positively inspired by the thought of new horizons at this time, together with unconventional ideas and a desire to do things your own way. It is not in your nature to be selfish, so you are able to get what you want, though without upsetting anyone on the way. In reality, your popularity is off the scale.

## 5 FRIDAY
*Moon Age Day 3    Moon Sign Virgo*

You should be willing to forego certain pleasures around now, in order to concentrate on matters that seem particularly important on a personal level. With little room for speculation, you should hang on to your money for the moment and also shelve a few social commitments until Sunday.

## 6 SATURDAY
*Moon Age Day 4    Moon Sign Virgo*

A few of the jobs you feel you must undertake today turn out to be hard work. There is no real reason why this should be the case but it might be best to simply rest for today. If at all possible, stick to things you like and undertake tasks one at a time for the best results.

# 7 SUNDAY
*Moon Age Day 5    Moon Sign Libra*

Affairs of the heart are well accented at present and the sign of Pisces is showing a spirited response to many aspects of life. Be careful of mechanical gadgets, one or two of which could be causing you minor problems around this time. The personal attitude of friends might be puzzling later in the day.

# 8 MONDAY
*Moon Age Day 6    Moon Sign Libra*

You are on top form when it comes to keeping the lines of communication with others open, and have no difficulty at all getting your message across to almost anyone. Advantages may arise from looking at life in a less than usual way. Anything curious, old or even odd is grist to your mill at the start of this week.

# 9 TUESDAY
*Moon Age Day 7    Moon Sign Libra*

There are likely to be better results from your financial efforts now, after a few days when this may not have seemed to be the case. However most of your efforts are not money-based at the moment. Friendships and deeper attachments occupy your time to a much greater extent than anything else.

# 10 WEDNESDAY
*Moon Age Day 8    Moon Sign Scorpio*

You will have to get one or two tedious jobs out of the way early in the day if you want to gain in the longer-term with social possibilities. Be careful about investing large sums of money around now and if it is necessary for you to sign any sort of document, do so after careful thought.

# 11 THURSDAY
*Moon Age Day 9    Moon Sign Scorpio*

You can get much from domestic matters around now, and indeed for a few days to come. Caring deeply about family members, you want to do all you can to please them, even if they don't always show the degree of gratitude that would please you. Your nature is what it is – you are just plain kind!

# 12 FRIDAY
*Moon Age Day 10    Moon Sign Sagittarius*

You have the ability at this stage of the month to find new solutions to old problems. Being particularly innovative and inspirational in the way you think, your frame of mind rubs off on those around you. All in all, this could turn out to be one of the most stimulating and interesting of days.

## 13 SATURDAY                    *Moon Age Day 11    Moon Sign Sagittarius*

Your mind works fast today but you might have a tendency to express yourself in ways that others find difficult to follow. It is worth taking the time to explain yourself fully and to make certain you don't give the wrong impression. Look out for an unexpected gift that could prove very welcome.

## 14 SUNDAY                    *Moon Age Day 12    Moon Sign Sagittarius*

The harder you work to improve your general financial situation at this time, the greater are the rewards that come in later. However, you also crave some excitement and will be quite unwilling to sit around the house all day, counting your money and checking your bank statements. Variety is important.

## 15 MONDAY                    *Moon Age Day 13    Moon Sign Capricorn*

In a professional sense this is a week during which you can get things moving in a very positive way. The secret in almost any situation now is 'don't wait to be asked'. You are sure of yourself to a greater extent than would normally be the case for your zodiac sign and others recognise this fact.

## 16 TUESDAY                    *Moon Age Day 14    Moon Sign Capricorn*

Disagreements are something you should avoid today or at the very least extricate yourself from as quickly as possible. If you really feel that someone needs taking to task leave this until tomorrow if you can. For now you need to be friends with as many people as possible and should avoid making waves.

## 17 WEDNESDAY                    *Moon Age Day 15    Moon Sign Aquarius*

Practical issues should go very much according to plan though personal contacts could be something of a disaster unless you given them proper attention. Be aware that planetary positions may adversely affect your time-keeping so keep an eye on your watch. Your mind is inclined to be all over the place today.

## 18 THURSDAY                    *Moon Age Day 16    Moon Sign Aquarius*

You now seem quite willing to work as hard as necessary in order to get exactly what you want from life. It's a pity that everyone else doesn't feel the same because you will practically have to bulldoze family members into doing their fair share today. Maybe you should threaten to go on strike!

## 19 FRIDAY
*Moon Age Day 17   Moon Sign Pisces*

Now things change significantly and you are going to find yourself in exactly the right frame of mind to take the world by storm. There are gains to be had both socially and romantically. Don't be too shy when in company and be willing to have your say. People are listening carefully.

## 20 SATURDAY
*Moon Age Day 18   Moon Sign Pisces*

Generally speaking you should find your level of luck extremely high at the moment. Although this won't incline you to go out and put your shirt on the horse running in the next race, you can afford to speculate a little more than usual. There could be some interesting compliments coming your way, too.

## 21 SUNDAY
*Moon Age Day 19   Moon Sign Aries*

Beware of taking too much for granted as far as your most intimate attachments are concerned. Rather than doing so you should put in that extra bit of effort that allows people to know for sure how you feel about them. Keep up your efforts to get ahead if you are at work, though not at any cost.

## 22 MONDAY
*Moon Age Day 20   Moon Sign Aries*

There isn't much doubt about your present organisational skills and you are equally efficient when arranging things at home or out in the wider world. Unfortunately there will be jobs to be done at the moment that you don't relish so the advice is to get them out of the way as early as you can, leaving more time later for fun.

## 23 TUESDAY
*Moon Age Day 21   Moon Sign Taurus*

You may be the expert when it comes to social relationships and could find ways of getting on well with even the most peculiar or awkward of people. This allows you to push forward in certain ways that have been blocked to you in the past. In addition you could discover skills you didn't know you had.

## 24 WEDNESDAY
*Moon Age Day 22   Moon Sign Taurus*

To certain other people you can appear to be indecisive when in reality you are merely showing a high degree of circumspection. You shouldn't worry about what those around you think today because you need to follow your own path and do things in the way your intuition tells you will work out best.

## 25 THURSDAY
*Moon Age Day 23    Moon Sign Gemini*

Your social life should be quite happy and stimulating under present trends, though there could seem to be something missing that you can't put your finger on. This temporary divine dissatisfaction is fairly typical of Pisces so maybe you shouldn't worry too much about it. There's no point in chasing rainbows – even for you.

## 26 FRIDAY
*Moon Age Day 24    Moon Sign Gemini*

The emphasis today is on appreciating all the good things life is presently offering you. Love, leisure and romance are all uppermost in your mind, even if none of them seem very likely on an average working day. Those Pisceans who are presently on holiday can make the most of these excellent planetary trends.

## 27 SATURDAY
*Moon Age Day 25    Moon Sign Gemini*

Although there are practical ups and downs to be dealt with at this time in most situations you know what you want and have a fairly good idea how to get it. Even good friends could prove to be just slightly irritating – mainly because they want to do things you don't. You can't have everything your own way, so compromise.

## 28 SUNDAY
*Moon Age Day 26    Moon Sign Cancer*

Others take note of your warmth, which adds to your attraction as far as they are concerned. For your own part you probably won't feel any different from usual – but it's what the world thinks that counts. Making new friends should be quite easy at the moment and you stretch out a hand to practically the whole world.

## 29 MONDAY
*Moon Age Day 27    Moon Sign Cancer*

Bringing a spirit of efficiency to your work should prove to be the most inspirational ability you possess at the moment. Even at home you could be tidier and more inclined to streamline tasks than you usually would. Family members may be willing to lend a hand at now – with a little prodding from you.

## 30 TUESDAY
*Moon Age Day 28    Moon Sign Leo*

This could be a fairly enjoyable but nevertheless quiet sort of day and might be best spent with your partner or family members close to home. If you have to travel try to make your journey more interesting by visiting a location that has a specific interest for you – maybe from a historical or personal point of view.

# 31 WEDNESDAY ☿

All the things that are happening at home could turn out to be just too frantic and demanding for your liking, which is why you could be spending more time with friends or colleagues today. There are times when you have to allow others to get on with things in their own sweet way and today turns out to be such an interlude.

# September 2016

## YOUR MONTH AT A GLANCE

$(+)$ = Opportunities are around    $(-)$ = Be on the defensive    $\bigcirc$ = Life is pretty ordinary

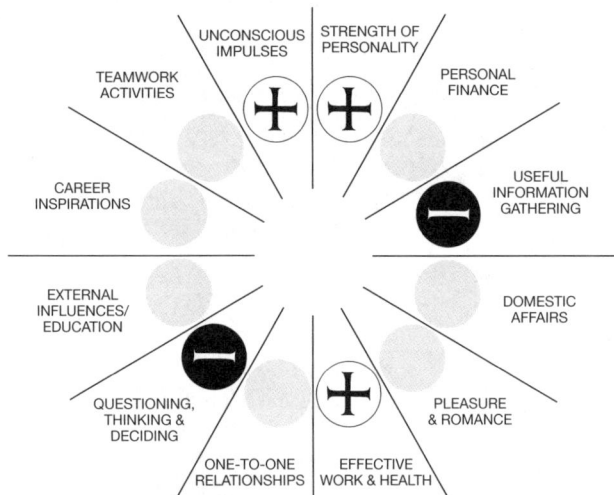

STRENGTH OF PERSONALITY

UNCONSCIOUS IMPULSES

TEAMWORK ACTIVITIES

PERSONAL FINANCE

CAREER INSPIRATIONS

USEFUL INFORMATION GATHERING

EXTERNAL INFLUENCES/ EDUCATION

DOMESTIC AFFAIRS

QUESTIONING, THINKING & DECIDING

PLEASURE & ROMANCE

ONE-TO-ONE RELATIONSHIPS

EFFECTIVE WORK & HEALTH

## SEPTEMBER HIGHS AND LOWS

*Here I show you how the rhythms of the Moon will affect you this month. Like the tide, your energies and abilities will rise and fall with its pattern. When it is above the centre line, go for it, when it is below, you should be resting.*

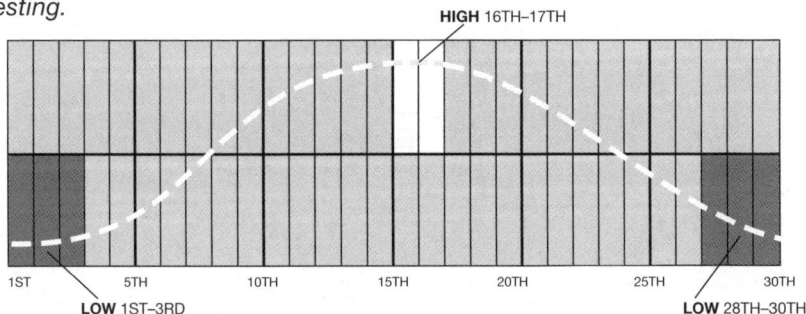

**HIGH** 16TH–17TH

1ST   5TH   10TH   15TH   20TH   25TH   30TH

**LOW** 1ST–3RD

**LOW** 28TH–30TH

## 1 THURSDAY ☿     *Moon Age Day 0   Moon Sign Virgo*

The lunar low might prevent the most exciting opportunities from taking place but you haven't much to fear from it right now. The fact is that you are so tied to what you know and what makes you feel most secure you are not likely to be painting the town red in any case. By Sunday things will start to change.

## 2 FRIDAY ☿     *Moon Age Day 1   Moon Sign Virgo*

It is possible that today you will have to deal with delays of one sort or another. Don't let them worry you too much because they are temporary. Be prepared to do things at a fairly steady rate and listen carefully to sound advice. By the evening you might be ready for a definite change of scene.

## 3 SATURDAY ☿     *Moon Age Day 2   Moon Sign Virgo*

Keep major plans up your sleeve until tomorrow. There is nothing to be gained at the moment from rushing things and you would be much better off simply taking some time out. Whilst you are in the mood for thinking, plan a special journey that will really please family members and especially your partner.

## 4 SUNDAY ☿     *Moon Age Day 3   Moon Sign Libra*

You need to watch out because you are more than a little outspoken at the moment and might end up saying something you will only regret in the longer-term. Think before you offer any opinion, especially to friends or relatives who you already know are rather too sensitive for their own good.

## 5 MONDAY ☿     *Moon Age Day 4   Moon Sign Libra*

You are affectionate and very considerate of others right now. This gets you plenty of attention in return and one or two people could be telling you how they really feel about you. Some Pisceans will be experiencing some wanderlust around now and will feel the need to get as much travel into their lives as possible.

## 6 TUESDAY ☿     *Moon Age Day 5   Moon Sign Scorpio*

The sooner you make decisions the better you will get on in a general sense. There is a slight tendency right now to sit on the fence and that won't really get you very far. Family arrangements might have to be left to others because you find yourself quite busy enough without them right now.

## 7 WEDNESDAY  ☿ *Moon Age Day 6   Moon Sign Scorpio*

This can be a period of improved communication with friends, though your personal attachments might be slightly more difficult to deal with. You are likely to focus on groups and associations with which you are choosing to become involved and this could lead to a whole new social circle.

## 8 THURSDAY  ☿ *Moon Age Day 7   Moon Sign Scorpio*

Your imagination and sensitivity is stimulated at present and you retain a slight desire to retire from the world. There might be no real reason to avoid this tendency because you can come out on the other side feeling refreshed and even keener to have a positive part to play. Situations will reverse themselves quicker than you think.

## 9 FRIDAY  ☿ *Moon Age Day 8   Moon Sign Sagittarius*

Much should be going according to plan now and this is the time during September when you need to take all your positive qualities and use them to your advantage. You are methodical but quick-thinking and posses exactly the right skills to get what you want from life. Enlisting support should be easy.

## 10 SATURDAY  ☿ *Moon Age Day 9   Moon Sign Sagittarius*

Deep emotions and issues from the past could easily surface around now and you might want to talk to one or two people in order to get these sorted out in your own mind. Don't put the blame on others for situations to which you contributed and wherever possible you should bury the hatchet.

## 11 SUNDAY  ☿ *Moon Age Day 10   Moon Sign Capricorn*

This is a time during which you can easily handle several different tasks at the same time. There are possible financial gains in the offing as well as interesting new projects of all kinds. Routines can be a bit of a bore, which is why you are quite willing to let others take some of the strain.

## 12 MONDAY  ☿ *Moon Age Day 11   Moon Sign Capricorn*

This is a day that is likely to be characterised by harmonious contact with most people but most especially those to whom you are related. At the same time you should find that the romantic potential of the day is good and you might be on the receiving end of an invitation or two that sound rather glamorous.

## 13 TUESDAY ☿ *Moon Age Day 12   Moon Sign Aquarius*

You should see your family as a source of fulfilment and strength, much along the lines of the astrological trends that were surrounding you yesterday. If you travel far it will be because arrangements to do so were made some time ago and even young Pisceans will be anxious to be with family members.

## 14 WEDNESDAY ☿ *Moon Age Day 13   Moon Sign Aquarius*

This would be a good time to make progress with any sort of DIY project. Once again you feel the need to be in or around your home but the practical side of your nature is also being stimulated. From something as simple as decorating, right up to the thought of an extension, you are in the market to get things done.

## 15 THURSDAY ☿ *Moon Age Day 14   Moon Sign Aquarius*

Certain feelings can be difficult to express positively and you are now slightly prone to moodiness, which ought to be avoided at all costs. Avoid disagreements, especially at home and keep your own counsel rather than giving offence that isn't necessary. It's very rare for Pisces to be grumpy but it does happen occasionally.

## 16 FRIDAY ☿ *Moon Age Day 15   Moon Sign Pisces*

**Along comes a physical peak, together with the need to break the bounds of the possible and even approach the impossible. Life should seem to be filled with certainties and you are even likely to speculate a little more than usual. Comfort and security will probably be the last things on your mind throughout the coming weekend.**

## 17 SATURDAY ☿ *Moon Age Day 16   Moon Sign Pisces*

**You can share interesting and mutually beneficial ideas and plans with almost anyone. You are still likely to be on top form and could find this to be the ideal sort of weekend. It somehow manages to bring together work and play and offers you the chance to look at new interests and activities.**

## 18 SUNDAY ☿ *Moon Age Day 17   Moon Sign Aries*

This is a favourable day on which to make a clean break with the past regarding some issue or other that has been on your mind for a while. You will also be very much in the market for a new sort of co-operation at the moment because things definitely do go better in pairs as far as you are concerned. Don't get too tied down with duties.

## 19 MONDAY ☿ *Moon Age Day 18   Moon Sign Aries*

Expanding your intellectual horizons today will be no bad thing. This is one of the best times imaginable for taking up new studies and academic interests. Life can be rather peculiar on occasions but you are going to be filled with a sense of enterprise and this would be the best time of all for some to think about self-employment.

## 20 TUESDAY ☿ *Moon Age Day 19   Moon Sign Taurus*

Today is potentially favourable when it comes to your career and getting yourself organised generally. At the same time there are probably social invitations in the offing and you might have to think hard before you get involved in too many things at the same time. Still, being spoilt for choice isn't that much of a problem and you'll cope somehow.

## 21 WEDNESDAY ☿ *Moon Age Day 20   Moon Sign Taurus*

You can probably benefit from the good advice of a friend but you do need to be fairly careful about following the suggestions of others, especially if the person concerned has some reason of their own for steering you down a particular path. It might seem as if you are up against it at work and you will have to pitch in early.

## 22 THURSDAY *Moon Age Day 21   Moon Sign Gemini*

There is likely to be a strong emphasis on the past and the way you view it in your own mind. However, you can't be expected to have a very balanced view of situations long gone and may have to rely on the memories of someone else to really get at the truth. In reality the only place you should be looking now is to the future.

## 23 FRIDAY *Moon Age Day 22   Moon Sign Gemini*

There is definite warmth in all your emotional dealings with the world at large and the fact that you are expressing your true feelings about everything will certainly help when it comes to personal attachments. Today is also good for joint financial matters and for getting to grips with a slightly sticky situation concerning friendships.

## 24 SATURDAY *Moon Age Day 23   Moon Sign Cancer*

All forms of intellectual activity are inclined to appeal to you today and you willingly set your mind to solving problems – some of which you are deliberately creating just for the sake of the exercise. It has rarely been easier to get your point of view across to others than it is at the moment and you can even talk to superiors with confidence.

## 25 SUNDAY
*Moon Age Day 24    Moon Sign Cancer*

Domestic issues should be working generally well for you now but if you feel even remotely bored by any aspect of your life, this is the moment to pep it up in some way. You remain generally happy with your lot and will spend a great deal of your time trying to make those around you as satisfied as you are.

## 26 MONDAY
*Moon Age Day 25    Moon Sign Leo*

Explore your creative side at every opportunity today and show just how stylish you can be when you have to involve yourself in public situations. It's worth going that extra yard with your appearance at the moment because people are looking at you more and will formulate many of their opinions upon first impressions.

## 27 TUESDAY
*Moon Age Day 26    Moon Sign Leo*

This is a time of personal regeneration when certain issues come to an end and are replaced by more modern concepts and ideas. It may take you all your time at present to keep up with new technology and it is likely that you will have to seek out some assistance if you want to know more than the basics regarding some new gadget.

## 28 WEDNESDAY
*Moon Age Day 27    Moon Sign Virgo*

Look to new options for change and growth and don't be held back by the sort of people who are always naturally pessimistic in any case. You need to do those things that specifically please you and which you know will eventually be in everyone's best interests. A new and more enterprising phase could be developing for some Pisceans.

## 29 THURSDAY
*Moon Age Day 28    Moon Sign Virgo*

This is likely to be a much quieter day and since the lunar low is preventing you from making the sort of progress you were starting to take for granted, you may have to work that much harder to gain your objectives. If practical matters can be left alone for a couple of days you might be well advised to put them aside.

## 30 FRIDAY
*Moon Age Day 0    Moon Sign Virgo*

Avoid pushing too hard today because you won't get what you want and will only exhaust yourself trying. Instead, clear the decks for the action that you will be able to take later, and also try to enjoy some rest and relaxation. It is easier for Pisces to adapt to the rhythm of the stars and be guided by them than it is for most other signs of the zodiac.

# October
### 2016

## Your Month at a Glance

⊕ = Opportunities are around    ⊖ = Be on the defensive    ⬤ = Life is pretty ordinary

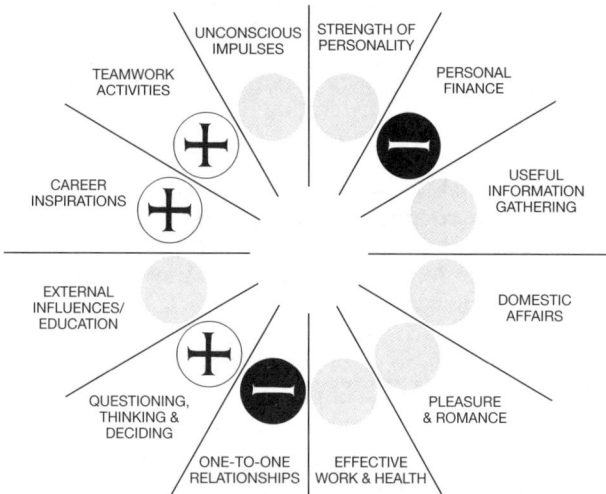

- UNCONSCIOUS IMPULSES
- STRENGTH OF PERSONALITY
- TEAMWORK ACTIVITIES
- PERSONAL FINANCE ⊖
- CAREER INSPIRATIONS ⊕
- USEFUL INFORMATION GATHERING
- EXTERNAL INFLUENCES/ EDUCATION
- DOMESTIC AFFAIRS
- QUESTIONING, THINKING & DECIDING ⊕
- ONE-TO-ONE RELATIONSHIPS ⊖
- PLEASURE & ROMANCE
- EFFECTIVE WORK & HEALTH
- TEAMWORK ACTIVITIES ⊕

## October Highs and Lows

*Here I show you how the rhythms of the Moon will affect you this month. Like the tide, your energies and abilities will rise and fall with its pattern. When it is above the centre line, go for it, when it is below, you should be resting.*

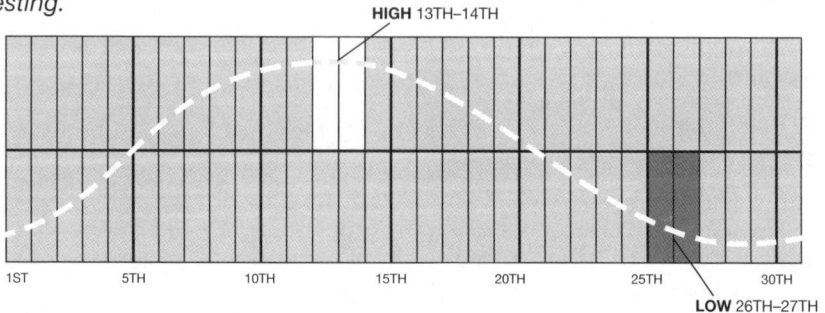

**HIGH** 13TH–14TH

1ST   5TH   10TH   15TH   20TH   25TH   30TH

**LOW** 26TH–27TH

## 1 SATURDAY
*Moon Age Day 1    Moon Sign Libra*

Personal relationships could prove quite demanding and you are likely to experience a few delays. Cut your losses with projects that are clearly not going to work out the way you would wish and get on with something new. Avoid feeling edgy by doing something that appeals to you personally.

## 2 SUNDAY
*Moon Age Day 2    Moon Sign Libra*

Avoid giving the impression that you know things you don't because there is a danger that you could come unstuck as a result. The best way forward is using the more modest approach that is usually so much a part of your nature. That gets people on your side and makes sure you receive any assistance you might need.

## 3 MONDAY
*Moon Age Day 3    Moon Sign Scorpio*

Emotionally and romantically there are now some significant high spots to be enjoyed. You should be feeling much more contented with your lot generally and won't easily be put off when you aim for something that is very important to you. Your confidence is gradually growing and material gains are likely.

## 4 TUESDAY
*Moon Age Day 4    Moon Sign Scorpio*

A matter close to home could turn out to be slightly disappointing but in a way this doesn't matter because your mind is turning outward to a much greater extent than might have been possible for a while. Misunderstandings should be avoided because they can spark off totally unnecessary rows.

## 5 WEDNESDAY
*Moon Age Day 5    Moon Sign Scorpio*

Consider a particular course of action carefully because you might make a mistake if you rush into anything too quickly. There are possible gains on the monetary front, though these demand that you take very decisive action over investments. Friends will be demanding but do offer you plenty of joy too.

## 6 THURSDAY
*Moon Age Day 6    Moon Sign Sagittarius*

This can be a good time to settle family issues once and for all and you remain in a positive and happy frame of mind. Issues that might have concerned you a great deal last week are now far less likely to cause you stress and yours is the most cheerful face to be found in most situations and places today.

## 7 FRIDAY
*Moon Age Day 7    Moon Sign Sagittarius*

Your domestic life is still rewarding but you won't be ignoring the needs of the wider world. Some Pisceans will now be finding that romance is the best area of life and there are likely to be invitations on the way that will delight you. You find yourself in a very creative and imaginative frame of mind.

## 8 SATURDAY
*Moon Age Day 8    Moon Sign Capricorn*

Your mind is filled with good ideas now and all the incentives that have been piling up inside you for some time are now showing themselves. Be bold in your approach and expect to succeed. There is a stop–start feel to certain issues but not if you charge your way through and refuse to accept second-best.

## 9 SUNDAY
*Moon Age Day 9    Moon Sign Capricorn*

You enjoy harmony and co-operation at the moment and will hate anything that gets in the way of your presently ordered mind. Avoid confusion by saying what you think from the word go and give yourself fully to whatever seems most appealing. This needs to be a Sunday that is spent at least partly thinking about yourself.

## 10 MONDAY
*Moon Age Day 10    Moon Sign Capricorn*

At work you are likely to be very efficient at the moment and easily able to tackle more than one job at once. When you are away from practical requirements you know how to have fun and won't have much trouble helping others to do the same. Personalities tend to come into your life around now.

## 11 TUESDAY
*Moon Age Day 11    Moon Sign Aquarius*

Your charm is well in evidence and you won't have very much of a problem getting round people. The fact is that you have a very attractive disposition and are always good to know. Add to this your natural tendency to be polite and the recipe is one that the world at large finds very appealing.

## 12 WEDNESDAY
*Moon Age Day 12    Moon Sign Aquarius*

You need to some emotional contact with very specific people today and should seek them out at the first possible opportunity. Getting to grips with the way your family members and even your friends are thinking might captivate you now but you will be very lucky if you find exactly the answers you are seeking.

## 13 THURSDAY
*Moon Age Day 13    Moon Sign Pisces*

It is now the professional and practical areas of life that offer the greatest potential rewards and you will be able to turn your mind outwards to the world at large. With greater vitality, less of a tendency to think in an insular way and terrific foresight, it's upward and onward with new projects and social possibilities.

## 14 FRIDAY
*Moon Age Day 14    Moon Sign Pisces*

Vital communications take place today and you certainly won't be backward at coming forward when it really matters. The sense of independence and determination is that much greater after such a quiet spell and you will want to ring every ounce of enjoyment out of situations that come along quite naturally.

## 15 SATURDAY
*Moon Age Day 15    Moon Sign Aries*

It is possible that you will discover today that it is better to adapt to the needs and desires of others, rather than to expect them to come to you. There are some very insecure people about and the right way to deal with them is to turn up the power of the caring qualities that are endemic to your nature.

## 16 SUNDAY
*Moon Age Day 16    Moon Sign Aries*

Now is a really good time to be taking stock and to decide whether the direction you are taking in life is really what you want. Dump some of the baggage and make sure that you focus on your own priorities. It's too easy for Pisces people to become fettered by an over-active sense of responsibility, sometimes for the whole world.

## 17 MONDAY
*Moon Age Day 17    Moon Sign Taurus*

On a slightly quieter day than of late you will have the time necessary to look deep into the heart of personal matters. In relationships you show yourself to be attentive and probing – so that those closest to you really do feel that you care. Don't take chances with money today, though you should be much luckier by tomorrow.

## 18 TUESDAY
*Moon Age Day 18    Moon Sign Taurus*

Certain situations demand a great deal of concentration today and you will be quite willing to put in that extra effort that means getting things right first time. It might seem as though you are somehow wasting valuable hours but in the longer-term it benefits you no end not to have to revisit situations more than once.

## 19 WEDNESDAY
*Moon Age Day 19    Moon Sign Gemini*

Socially speaking there isn't any doubt that you are going to be in great demand – so much so that it might be awkward trying to do everything that is expected of you. You need to balance out public obligations and personal desires, whilst at the same time finding moments during which you can reassure and help family members.

## 20 THURSDAY
*Moon Age Day 20    Moon Sign Gemini*

It's time to prune down parts of your life that are growing out of control – and in this way to allow the sun to shine in. October might seem a strange time for any sort of spring clean but that's what the planets are saying. There are times ahead that are going to demand your full attention and a less cluttered approach to life.

## 21 FRIDAY
*Moon Age Day 21    Moon Sign Cancer*

If others show themselves to have strong opinions today, yours are going to be stronger still. When friends or colleagues insist on arguing you can shout louder – though of course that is something you will avoid if you can. The simple fact is that you won't be put upon by anyone just now and will be quick to defend yourself.

## 22 SATURDAY
*Moon Age Day 22    Moon Sign Cancer*

You may feel that it would be sensible to simplify your life in some way – in fact in as many ways as proves to be possible. Travelling light is what suits Pisces best, but you also insist on picking up so much baggage as you go along. Every so often you dump some of the surplus load and boy do you feel better as a result!

## 23 SUNDAY
*Moon Age Day 23    Moon Sign Leo*

A personal attachment should prove to be very reassuring today and offers you the chance to say something that has been on your mind for a while. Don't try to crowd too many jobs into too short a time or you could end up doing everything badly. Take life one step at a time until tomorrow, when general trends are looking better.

## 24 MONDAY
*Moon Age Day 24    Moon Sign Leo*

Be accommodating when it comes to the opinions that other people hold and don't try to enforce your regimes on to people who are obviously reluctant. It's hard enough keeping your own life on track, without trying to do so for everyone else. Pisces could tend to be a little bossy at the moment and that's something you need to avoid.

## 25 TUESDAY
*Moon Age Day 25     Moon Sign Leo*

A stimulating force is at work as you take a more expansive approach to life in general. Desire for the new and the unusual is especially strong at present and you will be moving heaven and earth in order to open up new avenues and exciting horizons. Why not opt for a long journey in the near future? The planets show it to be a good option.

## 26 WEDNESDAY
*Moon Age Day 26     Moon Sign Virgo*

You might be having just a little difficulty in keeping pace with the latest developments, especially where technology is concerned. This is probably caused by the lunar low but rest assured that this is likely to be your only problem because you are well protected by a host of positive planetary positions and aspects.

## 27 THURSDAY
*Moon Age Day 27     Moon Sign Virgo*

Don't believe everything you hear today because there are people around who seem to have a vested interest in only offering a part of the truth. As long as you use your intuition this is not likely to be too much of a problem and you can tell disreputable types almost the moment you lay your eyes upon them.

## 28 FRIDAY
*Moon Age Day 28     Moon Sign Libra*

You will prefer to be mostly on the move today and can make this a special sort of Friday. Getting involved in more than one major project is not only likely at the moment it's virtually mandatory. Nothing is too much trouble if you know that your efforts now are going to mean more of what you really want in the weeks to come.

## 29 SATURDAY
*Moon Age Day 29     Moon Sign Libra*

Personal and business encounters with others are likely to turn out quite favourably under present trends but beware because there are one or two people around who you won't get on with very well. In all probability this isn't your fault but to avoid feelings of guilt later you should stay away from arguments with anyone today.

## 30 SUNDAY
*Moon Age Day 0     Moon Sign Libra*

This is an excellent day to start something new and to be in charge of your own destiny. Everything is likely to be working for you except the slight feeling that certain other people want to tell you how you should live your life. Make it quite plain, in your usual tactful way that you know exactly what you want.

## 31 MONDAY

Maybe you should now be slightly less sensitive to what are, after all, the casual remarks of other people. It could seem as if these are directed at you but in reality you may simply be over-analysing. Be cool, calm and collected in all situations and laugh off any setbacks because these are likely to be nothing to worry about.

# November

2016

## YOUR MONTH AT A GLANCE

⊕ = Opportunities are around   ⊖ = Be on the defensive   ⬤ = Life is pretty ordinary

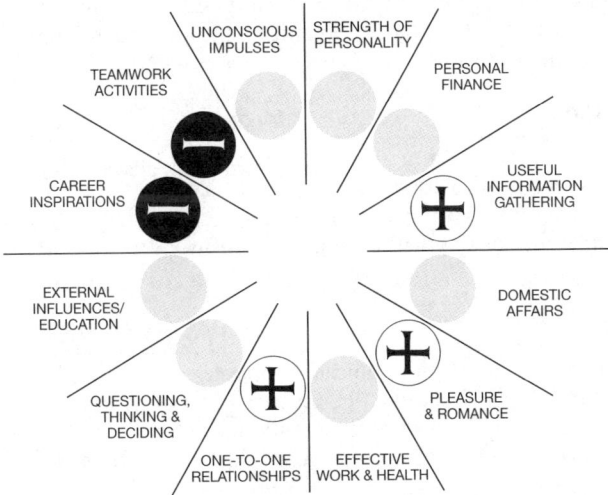

- UNCONSCIOUS IMPULSES
- STRENGTH OF PERSONALITY
- TEAMWORK ACTIVITIES
- PERSONAL FINANCE
- CAREER INSPIRATIONS ⊖
- USEFUL INFORMATION GATHERING ⊕
- EXTERNAL INFLUENCES/ EDUCATION
- DOMESTIC AFFAIRS
- QUESTIONING, THINKING & DECIDING ⊕
- PLEASURE & ROMANCE
- ONE-TO-ONE RELATIONSHIPS
- EFFECTIVE WORK & HEALTH

## NOVEMBER HIGHS AND LOWS

*Here I show you how the rhythms of the Moon will affect you this month. Like the tide, your energies and abilities will rise and fall with its pattern. When it is above the centre line, go for it, when it is below, you should be resting.*

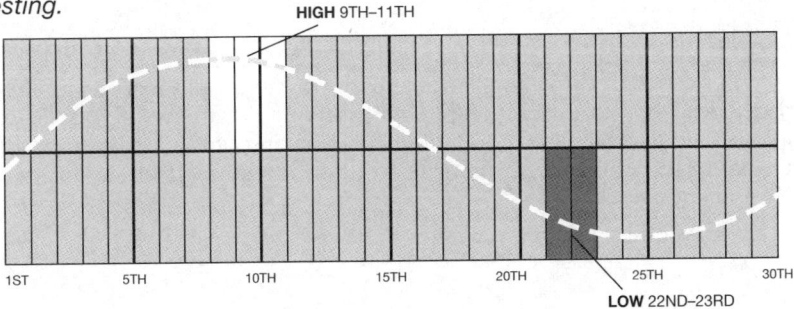

**HIGH** 9TH–11TH

1ST   5TH   10TH   15TH   20TH   25TH   30TH

**LOW** 22ND–23RD

## 1 TUESDAY
*Moon Age Day 2    Moon Sign Scorpio*

The emphasis today will probably be on social gatherings and you revel in the company of like-minded people. Places of entertainment appeal to you at the moment and you have what it takes to make the best possible impression on others. Stay away from situations that could prove to be embarrassing.

## 2 WEDNESDAY
*Moon Age Day 3    Moon Sign Sagittarius*

You will have the chance to make new friends today and to influence situations. A love affair could prove to be quite satisfying and you have a slight tendency to display the more dreamy side of your nature. Creative potential is especially good and you might be looking to make changes in and around your home.

## 3 THURSDAY
*Moon Age Day 4    Moon Sign Sagittarius*

Your love life is still enriching and might represent the best area on which to concentrate right now. Today has a great deal of potential and is especially useful when it comes to getting on with jobs that have been waiting for a while. You work away with a smile and know how to enlist the support of others.

## 4 FRIDAY
*Moon Age Day 5    Moon Sign Sagittarius*

There seem to be a good many things happening to you at the moment and once again your love life could be the focus of your attention. Maybe you are feeling particularly adored at the moment or it could be that some of the compliments you receive are coming from directions you didn't expect.

## 5 SATURDAY
*Moon Age Day 6    Moon Sign Capricorn*

The accent is on fun and romance in equal quantities. Your creative potential is good and allies itself to good organisational skills. Although you will find that there is plenty to do, you undertake it in a cheerful and positive way. Co-operative ventures are especially well-starred around this time.

## 6 SUNDAY
*Moon Age Day 7    Moon Sign Capricorn*

You tend to stick to those people who share your enthusiasm at the moment and that leads to some very happy and satisfying situations. If you are self employed this could be a good time for thinking about expanding your potential in some way, or for getting some sound advice from people who are in the know.

## 7 MONDAY
*Moon Age Day 8    Moon Sign Aquarius*

There are new opportunities for romance, or if you are in a settled relationship you can find ways to pep up your love life. Get out and about if you can and try to visit somewhere you find stimulating and which offers food for thought. A dinner date this evening could prove to be extremely interesting so organise one.

## 8 TUESDAY
*Moon Age Day 9    Moon Sign Aquarius*

Not everyone is likely to be sharing the high spirits that are so much a part of your nature at the moment and as a result you might have to tone things down just a little. Never mind, there will always be someone who is pleased to meet you on your own terms and to take joy from your present state of mind.

## 9 WEDNESDAY
*Moon Age Day 10    Moon Sign Pisces*

**The green light is on and success lies around every single corner. With the lunar high supporting your efforts and with masses of enthusiasm, this could turn out to be a highly promising day. You won't take kindly to rules and regulations and have a definite desire to do things your own way whenever possible.**

## 10 THURSDAY
*Moon Age Day 11    Moon Sign Pisces*

**You can double your luck today by simply being in the right place at the right time. It is unlikely that anything much will hold you back and you exhibit great determination when it matters the most. What is best about today is the way you react to situations that might sometimes take the wind out of your sails.**

## 11 FRIDAY
*Moon Age Day 12    Moon Sign Pisces*

**Now you can move ahead very effectively and should be much happier with your lot in life generally. This is a potentially productive Friday and offers you the chance to meet new people and to travel to places you have not seen before. There's something quite old-fashioned about you now but others find it attractive.**

## 12 SATURDAY
*Moon Age Day 13    Moon Sign Aries*

This is a time when you can appreciate the spirit of co-operation to the full. You are a real team player now and want to do as much as you can to support others. Keep up your present efforts to help younger family members, even if the level of appreciation coming back at you isn't quite what you might have hoped.

## 13 SUNDAY
*Moon Age Day 14    Moon Sign Aries*

There are challenges coming along to assault your ego at this stage of November. These could arrive from a number of different directions and you need to deal with each one on its own terms. None of this matters too much because you are efficient, hard working and keen to make real progress right now.

## 14 MONDAY
*Moon Age Day 15    Moon Sign Taurus*

The emotional side of life is likely to dominate today and you will find that intimate relationships are the best of all. Although you are likely to be getting on well at work there is a dreamy side to your nature that makes you wander a little in your head. Confidence is steady but not overwhelming.

## 15 TUESDAY
*Moon Age Day 16    Moon Sign Taurus*

If there is ever a good time for financial speculation this is it. There are strong supporting planetary influences, which should be especially helpful in enabling you to see ahead. Travel needs careful handing though because any lack of organisation on your part could lead to cancellations or delays.

## 16 WEDNESDAY
*Moon Age Day 17    Moon Sign Gemini*

Social trends should work out fairly well for you but there is a chance that you could make a few unforced errors at first today. As the hours pass you should settle down more but by that time you could have found yourself repeating tasks multiple times. Don't get too frustrated and just accept that these interludes happen now and again.

## 17 THURSDAY
*Moon Age Day 18    Moon Sign Gemini*

A break from busy routines would clearly do you the world of good today but do you have sufficient time to please yourself? At the end of the day it's really down to deciding for yourself because nobody is forcing you to work so hard. Simply drop the reins for a while and let someone else do some of the driving.

## 18 FRIDAY
*Moon Age Day 19    Moon Sign Cancer*

Ordinary, everyday responsibilities are something you should be quite happy to take in your stride at present. You have the power to make your life more refined, cultured and comfortable and you won't take kindly today to anything you see as being sordid or unsavoury. There is a greater sense of tidiness about you at this time.

## 19 SATURDAY
*Moon Age Day 20    Moon Sign Cancer*

Avoid falling foul of others in arguments today. Not only are you now far more likely to be crossing swords with colleagues, you may also find that loved ones are also slightly difficult to deal with. The way round this possibility is to refuse to be in any way contentious and to let other people please themselves whenever possible.

## 20 SUNDAY
*Moon Age Day 21    Moon Sign Leo*

Now is the best time to pursue your own independent interests. You can't live other people's lives for them and right now you shouldn't even try to do so. New ideas pop into your head all the time at the moment and you have a tendency to turn these to your advantage. Just about anything you really want can be yours – with a little effort.

## 21 MONDAY
*Moon Age Day 22    Moon Sign Leo*

Fulfilment in your work now comes from the recognition you get from others. Colleagues and superiors alike should be telling you how talented you are and for once you might believe what they are saying. Keep a sense of proportion regarding a family argument, which isn't half as important as it might at first seem.

## 22 TUESDAY
*Moon Age Day 23    Moon Sign Virgo*

Your energy level is likely to be on the low side for a couple of days so if life is quiet in any case you won't let this trouble you. It won't be hard for you to carry on with jobs that could have seemed tedious only yesterday and you are in a good position to get ahead now, simply by working hard.

## 23 WEDNESDAY
*Moon Age Day 24    Moon Sign Virgo*

Your ability to control things is not likely to be particularly high right now and you often have to accept what you see as being second best. Comfort and security seem quite important but there is no need to panic if you can't make things at home work out the way you want. Even by tomorrow the world could look quite different.

## 24 THURSDAY
*Moon Age Day 25    Moon Sign Libra*

Travel and intellectual interests are now even more accentuated now the Sun has ended its journey through your ninth house. You value your freedom in all senses today and will fight like a tiger if it seems that any aspect of personal choice is being taken away from you. Challenges are now part of your life and you relish them.

## 25 FRIDAY
*Moon Age Day 26    Moon Sign Libra*

An improvement in all things professional is not far away and today would be useful when it comes to looking and planning ahead in a career sense. In terms of your personal life there could be little tangible movement, except for the fact that your lover is, if anything, slightly vague and less inclined than usual to make decisions.

## 26 SATURDAY
*Moon Age Day 27    Moon Sign Libra*

Some fairly unusual opportunities to make new friends may arise and you may find yourself getting together with the sort of people who are going to be very advantageous to you in the not too distant future. Success comes from the written word and from communications that arrive via technology such as computers and mobile phone texts.

## 27 SUNDAY
*Moon Age Day 28    Moon Sign Scorpio*

You seem to have all the drive and energy you could possibly need today but that won't get you everything you want. Sometimes a little intuition is worth any amount of practical talent and when it comes to seeing through others right now you are at your very best. You radiate confidence and that proves to be important.

## 28 MONDAY
*Moon Age Day 29    Moon Sign Scorpio*

Happy social encounters are likely to continue and it looks as though you are coming to the end of something that has been a slight trial to you for a while now. This should leave your horizons uncluttered and you are coming to a period when it would be sensible to spend a little time thinking about what you intend to do next.

## 29 TUESDAY
*Moon Age Day 0    Moon Sign Sagittarius*

Superiors are likely to be well disposed towards you this week so you may as well ask for something you have wanted for a while. This could be more than a simple raise and might have something to do with your ambitions for the future. Working in partnerships would be good under present trends but finances are slightly variable.

## 30 WEDNESDAY
*Moon Age Day 1    Moon Sign Sagittarius*

Organise your personal schedule as well as you can or you could run into some difficulties today – mainly born out of untidiness or rushing too much. One area of your life that looks extremely settled and happy is romance. There are words of affection passing back and forth today and a few of them could be unexpected.

# December

2016

## YOUR MONTH AT A GLANCE

⊕ = Opportunities are around    ⊖ = Be on the defensive    ⬤ = Life is pretty ordinary

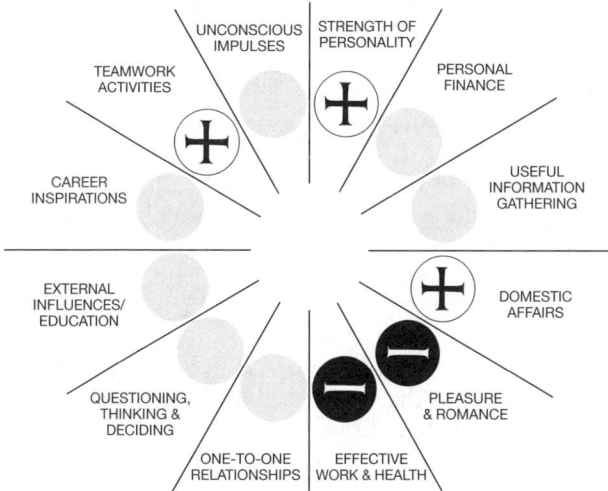

- UNCONSCIOUS IMPULSES
- STRENGTH OF PERSONALITY
- TEAMWORK ACTIVITIES
- PERSONAL FINANCE
- CAREER INSPIRATIONS
- USEFUL INFORMATION GATHERING
- EXTERNAL INFLUENCES/ EDUCATION
- DOMESTIC AFFAIRS
- QUESTIONING, THINKING & DECIDING
- PLEASURE & ROMANCE
- ONE-TO-ONE RELATIONSHIPS
- EFFECTIVE WORK & HEALTH

## DECEMBER HIGHS AND LOWS

*Here I show you how the rhythms of the Moon will affect you this month. Like the tide, your energies and abilities will rise and fall with its pattern. When it is above the centre line, go for it, when it is below, you should be resting.*

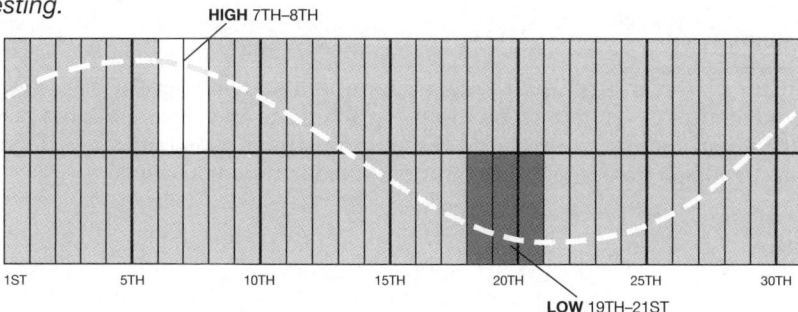

**HIGH** 7TH–8TH

1ST    5TH    10TH    15TH    20TH    25TH    30TH

**LOW** 19TH–21ST

## 1 THURSDAY
*Moon Age Day 2    Moon Sign Sagittarius*

Co-operation is required today if you are going to avoid getting into problems that are mostly brought about because of your ego. When the sign of Pisces is being its usual humble self there is no difficulty but at the moment you are so sure that you are right you probably won't give any ground at all.

## 2 FRIDAY
*Moon Age Day 3    Moon Sign Capricorn*

Your practical advancement is good and there is strong support for all your ideas. As the day advances you could find yourself listening too much to gossip and this is something that should be avoided. What is really good today is your ability to overturn obstacles that once seemed insurmountable.

## 3 SATURDAY
*Moon Age Day 4    Moon Sign Capricorn*

Working with others in almost any capacity turns out to be most fortunate today. That famous co-operative spirit is once again in evidence and you are a real mover and shaker at present. There should also be time for fun, which is just as important as the practical side of life. Combining the two isn't out of the question.

## 4 SUNDAY
*Moon Age Day 5    Moon Sign Aquarius*

This would be a fine time to make improvements at home and to get on with them as quickly as possible. Finances could look slightly stronger than over the past few days and that might be part of the reason you are willing to spend on domestic matters. Routines can be fun but there are moments when you want to push the bounds of the possible.

## 5 MONDAY
*Moon Age Day 6    Moon Sign Aquarius*

Take the initiative in social situations today because romance could be in the air. You may find yourself in the company of just the right people who can help you push forward in some important way. Recognising a blessing when it comes along may not be easy just now as some of them are deeply disguised.

## 6 TUESDAY
*Moon Age Day 7    Moon Sign Aquarius*

The time has come to handle bigger responsibilities, whether these are in the home or at work. A gradual build-up of confidence and capabilities has been evident throughout the year and reaches something of a climax now. Don't doubt yourself because you are far more capable than you think.

## 7 WEDNESDAY
*Moon Age Day 8    Moon Sign Pisces*

The lunar high can prove very important this time around. In material affairs you know what you want and have a very good idea how to go about getting it. Such is the strength of your nature at the moment that very few people will stand in your way. It's time to make hay while the sun shines.

## 8 THURSDAY
*Moon Age Day 9    Moon Sign Pisces*

Major decisions that are made now have a lasting part to play in your life and since you are so sensible, they are likely to be very far-reaching. There might not be quite as much time to spend with relatives as you would like but such is your energy that you manage to do many different things at once.

## 9 FRIDAY
*Moon Age Day 10    Moon Sign Aries*

Whilst it is unlikely there is anything standing in your way today, people who are clearly stressed could subject you to the odd temperamental outburst. Do what you can to help them out, even if all you can manage is to have a chat with them. Your naturally sympathetic tendencies are definitely called into play right now.

## 10 SATURDAY
*Moon Age Day 11    Moon Sign Aries*

It has probably only now occurred to you that this is already the second week of December and that means Christmas is only a stone's throw away. Don't use this fact as an excuse to panic because you probably have more organised than you realise. In any case a degree of last-minute planning should make the festivities even more enjoyable for a Piscean.

## 11 SUNDAY
*Moon Age Day 12    Moon Sign Taurus*

This is undoubtedly the right time of the month to take overall responsibility for your own ideas. If you insist on sharing everything with others, they will get the credit for something to which they have no right. Pisces is not inclined to be selfish but there is a limit and if you stop to think about things you will realise you've reached it.

## 12 MONDAY
*Moon Age Day 13    Moon Sign Taurus*

You may enjoy greater intellectual freedom at the start of this week. It is possible that someone who has refused to offer you assistance in the past is now more than willing to lend a hand. The problem is likely to be working out how to tell them that you have chosen your own way forward. Use some tact and diplomacy.

## 13 TUESDAY
*Moon Age Day 14    Moon Sign Gemini*

When it comes to professional matters you now have such a persuasive manner that you could probably get more or less anything you want. Don't wait to be asked in any situation where it is clear to you that a specific action needs to be taken. By the time you have qualified your thoughts with someone else it might be too late.

## 14 WEDNESDAY
*Moon Age Day 15    Moon Sign Gemini*

In amongst the start of the December festivities trends suggest that you will be put on some sort of pedestal – most likely by more than one person. You are at your very best in social situations and positively glow with good health and vitality. This is a good time for Pisces. It isn't difficult to be the centre of attention today.

## 15 THURSDAY
*Moon Age Day 16    Moon Sign Cancer*

Exercise a little care today because it looks as though many Pisceans are burning the candle at both ends and in the middle, too. A few minutes spent relaxing would do you the world of good. Communication with friends and colleagues is now likely to be quite stimulating. What's more it should also be highly productive.

## 16 FRIDAY
*Moon Age Day 17    Moon Sign Cancer*

Emotional matters could seem somewhat tense and extra effort is necessary if you want to sort out hiccups in relationships. This will only be possible if other people want to get involved and of course it takes two to tango. Away from the emotional arena you should find that financial matters are sorting themselves out.

## 17 SATURDAY
*Moon Age Day 18    Moon Sign Leo*

Pisces people who work at the weekend should now discover that they are taking on new responsibilities, some of which can seem confusing at first. With a little time and effort you can master something that would have seemed impossible a few months ago. This is a time of challenge, both inside and outside your home.

## 18 SUNDAY
*Moon Age Day 19    Moon Sign Leo*

You can only really prosper if you look ahead. Even though this is a naturally nostalgic time of the year there is no future in the past – either yours or anyone else's. Don't harp on today about things that are dead and gone in your life. If you are a little low today you can thank the approaching lunar low for this.

# 19 MONDAY
*Moon Age Day 20    Moon Sign Virgo*

This is not a time for new ambitions or for taking leaps forward. The lunar low tends to sap your strength a little but it's good to know that you will get this interlude well and truly out of the way before Christmas arrives. Just do what is expected of you and allow others to take some of the strain.

# 20 TUESDAY ☿
*Moon Age Day 21    Moon Sign Virgo*

Another day during which you will stand and watch more than take part. This does give you time to think, which is always useful for your zodiac sign. Winning races comes as second-nature once today is out of the way but in the meantime you might be better off planning for future events.

# 21 WEDNESDAY ☿
*Moon Age Day 22    Moon Sign Virgo*

You could be required to make some vital last minute changes in the work department. It is possible that others are not pulling their weight as much as they might and that could mean more responsibility for you. With only a few days to go you will most likely be attending to festive requirements.

# 22 THURSDAY ☿
*Moon Age Day 23    Moon Sign Libra*

You could be slightly caught between the desire to get on in a practical way, whilst at the same time thinking seriously about what Christmas has in store for you but there are ways and means to fit everything in if you think about it. Keeping busy is the way forward today and there won't be much standing in your way.

# 23 FRIDAY ☿
*Moon Age Day 24    Moon Sign Libra*

Today brings some contentment that details have been dealt with but it's a pound to a penny you've forgotten something. Your own ambitions are now particularly strong and they could get in the way of the wishes of people in your vicinity. That can't be helped because at the end of the day we all have to look out for number one.

# 24 SATURDAY ☿
*Moon Age Day 25    Moon Sign Scorpio*

It appears that Christmas Eve will find you giving more energy than ever to your partner and family matters generally. This is ideal for the sign of Pisces and you revel in the happiness you are able to bring to others. Don't forget your friends, one or two of whom are making social demands on you at some time today.

## 25 SUNDAY ☿ *Moon Age Day 26 Moon Sign Scorpio*

Even with the Christmas festivities taking place at home, the urge to travel is strengthened by present planetary positions. You can settle for a while but you need to be physically active at some stage today, so Christmas afternoon in front of the television is much less likely for you than it might sometimes be.

## 26 MONDAY ☿ *Moon Age Day 27 Moon Sign Scorpio*

Your movements might be slightly restricted but that's something you manage to work around. From a social point of view Boxing Day is likely to be a very positive time for you. Of course you will be expected to mix and mingle with others on a public holiday but for now you actively want to be involved as much as possible.

## 27 TUESDAY ☿ *Moon Age Day 28 Moon Sign Sagittarius*

Maybe you are not thinking things through as clearly as you normally do or it could be that you are just slightly less sensitive. Be careful that you don't expect something from a friend that is going to be very difficult if not impossible for them to deliver. Look at matters carefully and leave room for flexibility.

## 28 WEDNESDAY ☿ *Moon Age Day 29 Moon Sign Sagittarius*

Family gatherings are well-starred and will be much more successful if you get the chance to go somewhere different. There is one overriding desire within the sign of Pisces at the moment and that is the need for a change of scene. It doesn't matter if this is only ten minutes down the road. A change is certainly as good as a rest to your sign now.

## 29 THURSDAY ☿ *Moon Age Day 0 Moon Sign Capricorn*

This could turn out to be the quietest day across the Christmas holidays. Spending time with loved ones is definitely to be recommended today. Not only do they give you the emotional support you always need but they can talk over shared experiences from the past that are presently contributing to your feelings about the future.

## 30 FRIDAY ☿ *Moon Age Day 1 Moon Sign Capricorn*

This would be a great day for a shopping spree or for travelling to see something you have been promising yourself for ages. Today signifies a period when just about anything could happen. Make an early start with all-important activities but don't do more than you have to in order to get the result you want in any particular situation.

# 31 SATURDAY   ☿

If you are putting yourself about now you are definitely following the astrological trends that are most positive in your solar chart. Activities of almost any sort are well-starred but standing still certainly isn't. You have a low boredom threshold at the moment so keep busy and enjoy the New Year celebrations.

# How to Calculate Your Rising Sign

**M**ost astrologers agree that, next to the Sun Sign, the most important influence on any person is the Rising Sign at the time of their birth. The Rising Sign represents the astrological sign that was rising over the eastern horizon when each and every one of us came into the world. It is sometimes also called the Ascendant.

Let us suppose, for example, that you were born with the Sun in the zodiac sign of Libra. This would bestow certain characteristics on you that are likely to be shared by all other Librans. However, a Libran with Aries Rising would show a very different attitude towards life, and of course relationships, than a Libran with Pisces Rising.

For these reasons, this book shows how your zodiac Rising Sign has a bearing on all the possible positions of the Sun at birth. Simply look through the Aries table opposite.

As long as you know your approximate time of birth the graph will show you how to discover your Rising Sign.

Look across the top of the graph of your zodiac sign to find your date of birth, and down the side for your birth time (I have used Greenwich Mean Time). Where they cross is your Rising Sign. Don't forget to subtract an hour (or two) if appropriate for Summer Time.

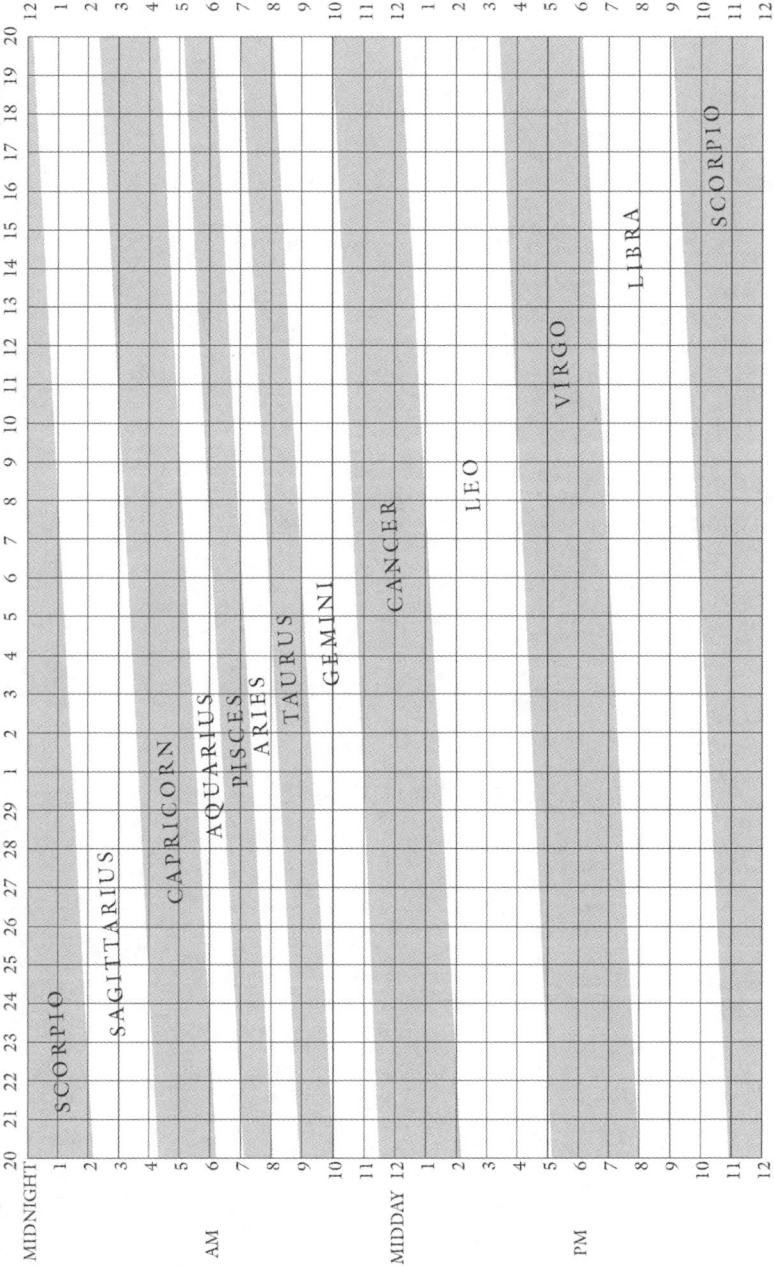

Chart showing rising signs for Pisces across the period FEBRUARY 20 to MARCH 20, with times running from MIDNIGHT through AM, MIDDAY, PM back to 12. Zodiac bands shown include SCORPIO, SAGITTARIUS, CAPRICORN, AQUARIUS, PISCES, ARIES, TAURUS, GEMINI, CANCER, LEO, VIRGO, LIBRA and SCORPIO.

# THE ZODIAC, PLANETS AND CORRESPONDENCES

The Earth revolves around the Sun once every calendar year, so when viewed from Earth the Sun appears in a different part of the sky as the year progresses. In astrology, these parts of the sky are divided into the signs of the zodiac and this means that the signs are organised in a circle. The circle begins with Aries and ends with Pisces.

Taking the zodiac sign as a starting point, astrologers then work with all the positions of planets, stars and many other factors to calculate horoscopes and birth charts and tell us what the stars have in store for us.

The table below shows the planets and Elements for each of the signs of the zodiac. Each sign belongs to one of the four Elements: Fire, Air, Earth or Water. Fire signs are creative and enthusiastic; Air signs are mentally active and thoughtful; Earth signs are constructive and practical; Water signs are emotional and have strong feelings.

It also shows the metals and gemstones associated with, or corresponding with, each sign. The correspondence is made when a metal or stone possesses properties that are held in common with a particular sign of the zodiac.

Finally, the table shows the opposite of each star sign – this is the opposite sign in the astrological circle.

| Placed | Sign | Symbol | Element | Planet | Metal | Stone | Opposite |
|--------|------|--------|---------|--------|-------|-------|----------|
| 1 | Aries | Ram | Fire | Mars | Iron | Bloodstone | Libra |
| 2 | Taurus | Bull | Earth | Venus | Copper | Sapphire | Scorpio |
| 3 | Gemini | Twins | Air | Mercury | Mercury | Tiger's Eye | Sagittarius |
| 4 | Cancer | Crab | Water | Moon | Silver | Pearl | Capricorn |
| 5 | Leo | Lion | Fire | Sun | Gold | Ruby | Aquarius |
| 6 | Virgo | Maiden | Earth | Mercury | Mercury | Sardonyx | Pisces |
| 7 | Libra | Scales | Air | Venus | Copper | Sapphire | Aries |
| 8 | Scorpio | Scorpion | Water | Pluto | Plutonium | Jasper | Taurus |
| 9 | Sagittarius | Archer | Fire | Jupiter | Tin | Topaz | Gemini |
| 10 | Capricorn | Goat | Earth | Saturn | Lead | Black Onyx | Cancer |
| 11 | Aquarius | Waterbearer | Air | Uranus | Uranium | Amethyst | Leo |
| 12 | Pisces | Fishes | Water | Neptune | Tin | Moonstone | Virgo |